The AutoCAD for Windows Book

"Draw from Experience" to build your AutoCAD® library

COMPREHENSIVE AUTOCAD

- •Stellman/HARNESSING AUTOCAD
  (Release 12 with Simulator® Tutorial Disk Package)   ISBN 0-8273-5917-9
  (Release 12 with Project Exercise Disk)   ISBN 0-8273-5930-6
  (Release 11)   ISBN 0-8273-4685-9

- •Fuller/USING AUTOCAD
  (Release 12)   ISBN 0-8273-5838-5
  (Release 11)   ISBN 0-8273-5344-8

- •Kalameja/THE AUTOCAD TUTOR FOR ENGINEERING GRAPHICS
  (Release 12)   ISBN 0-8273-5914-4
  (Release 11)   ISBN 0-8273-5081-3

- •Rubenstein/AUTOCAD: THE DRAWING TOOL
  (Release 11)   ISBN 0-8273-4885-1

- •McGrew/EXPLORING THE POWER OF AUTOCAD
  (Release 10)   ISBN 0-8273-3694-2

AUTOLISP & CUSTOMIZING

- •Kramer/AUTOLISP PROGRAMMING FOR PRODUCTIVITY   ISBN 0-8273-5832-6

- •Tickoo/CUSTOMIZING AUTOCAD
  (Release 12)   ISBN 0-8273-5895-4
  (Release 11)   ISBN 0-8273-5041-4

ADVANCED AUTOCAD

- •Grabowski/AUTOCAD FOR WINDOWS   ISBN 0-8273-5581-5

- •Grabowski/THE SUCCESSFUL CAD MANAGER'S HANDBOOK   ISBN 0-8273-5233-6

AUTOCAD APPLICATIONS

- •Miller/AUTOCAD FOR THE APPAREL INDUSTRY   ISBN 0-8273-5224-7

GENERIC CADD

- •White/USING GENERIC CADD 6.0   ISBN 0-8273-5571-8

CAD REFERENCE

- •Grabowski/THE ILLUSTRATED AUTOCAD QUICK REFERENCE
  (Release 12)   ISBN 0-8273-5839-3
  (Release 11)   ISBN 0-8273-4820-7

To purchase, contact your local bookseller or write directly to:
Delmar Publishers Inc, 3 Columbia Circle Drive, P.O. Box 15015, Albany, NY 12212

The AutoCAD for Windows Book

Release 11 and 12

Ralph Grabowski

Delmar Publishers Inc.™

I(T)P™

NOTICE TO THE READER

Cover Credit: **Michael Speke**
Book Design: **Ralph H Grabowski**

Delmar Staff
Associate Editor: **Pamela Graul**
Project Development Editor: **Mary Beth Ray**
Production Coordinator: **Andrew Crouth**
Art and Design Coordinator: **Lisa L Bower**

For information, contact:
Delmar Publishers, Inc.
3 Columbia Circle, Box 15015,
Albany, NY 12212-5015

Printed in the United States of America
Published simultaneously in Canada by Nelson Canada,
a division of the Thompson Corporation.

1 2 3 4 5 6 7 8 9 10 XXX 00 99 98 97 96 95 94

Library of Congress Cataloging-in-Publication Data:
Grabowski, Ralph
    AutoCAD for Windows/Ralph Grabowski
        p. cm.
    Includes index.
    ISBN 0-8273-5581-5
    1. Computer Graphics. 2. AutoCAD for Windows. I. Title
T385.G69 1994
620'.0042'02855369—dc20

93—25856
CIP

Brief Contents

Section III: **Multimedia AutoCAD**

Section IV: **Programming AutoCAD**

Table of Contents

Section I: AutoCAD for Windows

Section II: Integrating AutoCAD

Section III: Multimedia AutoCAD

Section IV: Programming AutoCAD

Introduction

I n his warning message to Autodesk, "The Final Days," John Walker proclaimed Windows as the second revolution in computing—after IBM's introduction of the Personal Computer in 1981. He urged Autodesk to redirect its massive programming efforts toward producing Windows versions of its software, particularly AutoCAD. Less than a year later on March 1, 1992, Autodesk released AutoCAD for Windows Extension. AWE, as it is was known, had the distinction of being the first major CAD package released for the Windows operating system. This book is about AutoCAD for Windows Releases 11 and 12 and their differences from AutoCAD for DOS/386.

The Purpose of This Book

The AutoCAD for Windows Book tells you how to use AutoCAD with Windows. This book doesn't show you how to draw a line or plot a drawing. Instead, it tells you what is new and different about AcadWin from the DOS version of AutoCAD.

This book describes the differences between DOS and Windows versions of AutoCAD. Step-by-step tutorials show you how to use the special features of AcadWin. You find out about integrating AcadWin with other Windows applications and how to use the easy programming resources provided by the Windows environment.

The Audience for This Book

Instead of showing you how to draw a line more efficiently, this book will be of interest to four types of AutoCAD user:

▶ The curious who want to understand what AutoCAD for Windows is all about

▶ The CAD manager who needs to know how to integrate Windows-based AutoCAD with DOS-based AutoCAD

▶ The AutoCAD programmer who wants to get into the Windows-style of programming

▶ The Windows users who spends more time in other programs but needs to occasionally dip into CAD

I assume that you are already familiar with DOS, Windows, AutoCAD, and using a text editor. There are many other books on the market that deal with those basics.

Tips and Tutorials

In addition to describing AutoCAD for Windows, this book contains 48 tips and 37 step-by-step tutorials. The tips are separated from the text in their own boxes—that help you quickly find them. The tutorials describe how to use AutoCAD and Windows features in numbered steps, walking you through each mouse click, menu selection, and command entry.

As a further aid, all the shareware and sample drawings described in this book are available at a low cost direct from the author. Check the back of this book for the order form.

The Organization of this Book

This book is divided into four sections:

Section I: AutoCAD for Windows
The first section of the book looks at what is new and different about AutoCAD for Windows.

Chapter 1: A Quick Tour tells you what is new in AutoCAD for Windows Extension, contrasting and comparing AcadWin with the DOS version of AutoCAD Release 11.

Chapter 2: Windows Navigation describes how to get around in the Windows operating environment. Once you know how to use one Windows application, you are familiar with all other Windows applications.

Chapter 3: Display Processing shows the advantages and disadvantages to display-list processing. Tutorials describe how to use the Aerial View feature with its bird's-eye view and spyglass.

Section II: Integrating AutoCAD
One of the primary advantages to AcadWin is its ability to easily integrate its data with other Windows applications. This section describes how to use AutoCAD for Windows with other programs and utilities.

Chapter 4: The Windows Clipboard is the key to quick'n easy data transfer between Windows applications. This chapter includes three tutorials for transferring raster, vector, and text data.

Chapter 5: Integrating Applications shows how to use AcadWin with other major Windows applications packages.

Chapter 6: Object Linking and Embedding lets you create live links between AutoCAD and OLE-client applications.

Chapter 7: Helpful Software describes software that makes it easier the manage with Windows and AutoCAD on one computer.

Chapter 8: Windows Shareware tells you about eight great shareware programs for Windows. Most of free or cost less than $30. They are also available on the optional diskette.

Section III: Multimedia AutoCAD

The computing buzzword of the early 90's is "multimedia." AutoCAD for Windows is fully capable of sound and animation, as this section shows.

Chapter 9: Audio Notes is a tutorial in adding sound notes to AutoCAD drawings, then playing them back.

Chapter 10: Animating AutoCAD shows you how to energize AutoCAD 3D drawings with animation.

Chapter 11: Motion and Sound describes how to play back animations with the Windows v3.1 Media Player and how to edit WAV sound files.

Section IV: Programming AutoCAD

The most exciting aspect to Windows is how much easier—and cheaper—it makes customizing AutoCAD, from the new Tool Bar to the Visual Basic programming. This section contains tutorials to help you program AutoCAD, Windows-style.

Chapter 12: The Toolbar and Toolbox make it a snap to create macros on the fly. This chapter's step-by-step tutorials show you how, even if you have never programmed before.

Chapter 13: Dynamic Data Exchange is the powerful means Windows provides to automatically transfer data between Windows programs. This chapter tells you all about DDE and how to use it with the Microsoft Excel spreadsheet.

Chapter 14: Introduction to Visual Basic is about the Visual Basic programming environment, the new GUI-based and event-driven programming environment. Visual Basic lets you create programs written in Basic that look like real Windows applications.

Chapter 15: Programming with Visual Basic introduces you to the steps in writing a Visual Basic program and run it with AutoCAD.

Chapter 16: Autodesk Utilities describes supplemental files released by Autodesk and third-party programmers after AutoCAD for Windows came out.

Acknowledgements

Many people and companies helped to make this book possible. They include:

▸ Neele Johnston and Autodesk for providing timely copies of beta and released copies of AutoCAD for Windows Releases 11 and 12.

▸ Microsoft Canada, Image-In Inc, Computer Support Corp, Vermont Microsystems, ATI Technology and Autodesk Retail Products for providing hardware and software to support this project.

▸ My wife and family: Heather, Stefan, Heidi, and Katrina.

Ralph Grabowski
June 24, 1993
Abbotsford, BC

About the Author

R alph Grabowski is a free-lance writer and independent consultant based in Abbotsford, British Columbia. He has written about AutoCAD since 1985 and is the author of 12 books about computer-aided design. Ralph holds the position of CAD Series Editor for Delmar Publishers, is a Contributing Editor to Cadence magazine, and sits on the Review Board of InfoWorld magazine. He is the former Senior Editor of CADalyst, the first magazine for AutoCAD users. Ralph received his B.A.Sc. degree in Civil Engineering from the University of British Columbia.

SECTION I

AutoCAD for Windows

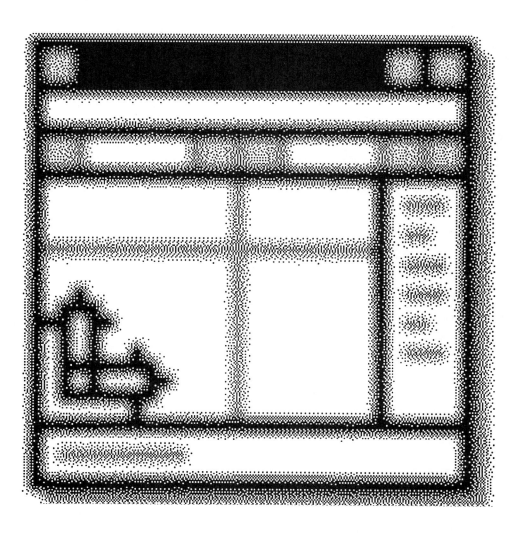

𝟙

The Quick Tour

utoCAD for Windows works identically to the DOS version of Release 12. All commands, AutoLISP routines, ADS applications, and extras—like AME solid modelling, ASE and ASI SQL links, and AVE rendering—work the same. The difference lies in the exciting features made possible by Windows. The Windows version of AutoCAD adds new ways to exchange data with other programs and makes effortless programming environments possible. This chapter provides a brisk excursion through 23 new and enhanced features, contrasting them with the DOS version of AutoCAD.

Executive Summary

AutoCAD Release 12 for Windows boasts the following 23 features:

New User Interface Enhancements
- Fast redraws, zooms, and pans
- Aerial view
- Scroll bars
- Digitizer support
- Find file
- Changed function keys

Enhanced AutoCAD Features
- Context-sensitive hyperlink help
- Independent text screen window
- On-the-fly configuration
- AVE Render
- ASVU

Enhanced Windows Features
- Multiple sessions
- Drag and drop
- Windows Clipboard
- Object linking and embedding

New Programming Features
- The Toolbar
- The Toolbox
- Iconic pop-down menus
- Macro metacharacters, AutoLISP functions, and ADS commands
- Dynamic data exchange
- Eight-bit character translation
- ODBC support
- ADS compiler support

The following pages present a summary of each new and enhanced feature, with the menu picks to access the feature.

Fast Redraws, Zooms, and Pans

▶ *First introduced in Release 12 for Windows*

AutoCAD Release 11 for Windows suffered from redraw speeds two to three times slower than AutoCAD for DOS/386. That made using AcadWin a painful and slow experience. To solve the problem, third-party developers wrote display-list drivers. These speed up redraws by up to 50 times, depending on the hardware and the drawing used.

For Release 12, Autodesk borrowed the third-party developers' idea and made display-list processing a part of the core technology. Sometimes, redraws, zooms and pans are actually faster in the Windows version than in the DOS/386 version of Release 12!

AutoCAD for Windows gives you two choices in speeding up the redraw speed: (1) display-list processing; (2) bypassing the Windows GDI (short for graphical device interface). By default, both options are turned on and, in most cases, you should leave them on for fastest display performance. Display-list processing works with all graphics boards supported by Windows. Bypassing the Windows GDI means less processing overhead imposed by the Windows operating environment.

▶ *How to access display-list processing:*
```
File | Configure
Select option 3, "Configure Video Display," then
select "Windows Accelerated Display Driver."
```

▶ *For more information on display-list processing, see Chapter 3.*

New Feature
Aerial View

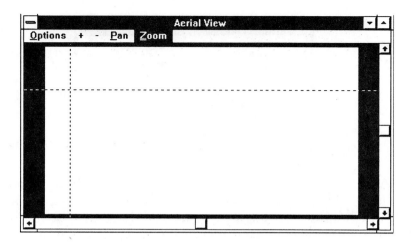

- *First introduced in AutoSketch for Windows*
- *Enhanced in AutoCAD Release 12 for Windows*

When you are working zoomed-in on an AutoCAD drawing, you may not always be sure where you are in the drawing. With version 2.5, AutoCAD added the Zoom Dynamic view to a road map to zoom and pan about the drawing. When AutoSketch for Windows was released, it sported an Aerial View—Autodesk's name for the bird's-eye view. The *bird's-eye view* is an independent display window that always shows the full extent of the drawing and lets you zoom and pan about the drawing; a rectangle shows the current view.

Autodesk added a dual-purpose Aerial View to Release 12 for Windows (see figure). Aerial View is both a bird's-eye view and as a spyglass. It floats anywhere on the Windows desktop. The *spyglass* is the inverse of the bird's-eye view, showing an enlarged view of the area under the cursor.

- *How to access Aerial View:*
  Command: **dsviewer**

- *For more information on the Aerial View, see Chapter 3.*

New Feature
Scroll Bars

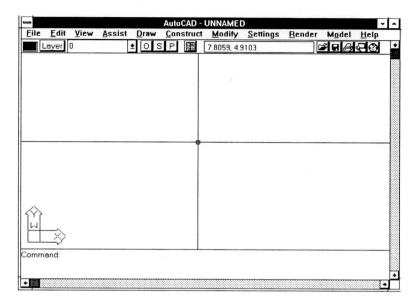

▸ *First introduced in AutoSketch v3 for DOS*

Many Windows applications let you pan around the screen by means of scroll bars. Scroll bars were first introduced by Autodesk in AutoSketch v3 for DOS. By clicking on the scroll bar, you pan about the drawing.

AutoCAD Release 12 for Windows has scroll bars but only with the non-display-list processing driver. It acts as a replacement to Aerial View, which does not work with the non-dlp driver. To use scroll bars, you must first configure AutoCAD with the plain "Windows driver."

▸ *How to access scroll bars:*
```
File | Preferences... | Scroll Bars
```

▸ *For more information on using scroll bars, see Chapter 2.*

Digitizer Support

- *First introduced in Release 10 for Macintosh*
- *Enhanced in AutoCAD Release 12 for Windows*

In earlier GUI versions of AutoCAD, Autodesk developed a "mole mode" that allowed a mouse and a digitizing tablet to co-exist. While you could run AutoCAD with just a mouse, you couldn't run it with just a digitizing tablet. The drawback was that you still had to have a mouse connected since the digitizer did not work in the rest of Windows.

Some digitizer manufacturers came up with mouse emulation for their tablets. For Release 12, Autodesk developed a new pointing device driver that lets a digitizing tablet work in Windows mouse mode (relative pointing) and AutoCAD digitizer mode (absolute picking).

- *How to access digitizer pointing mode:*
  ```
  File | Configure
  Select option 4, "Configure Digitizer."
  ```

TIP NUMBER 1
Summasketch Bug in Release 12

When AutoCAD for Windows Release 12 and 12c1 are configured with the Summasketch option of the DgSys.Dll system digitizer driver, there are times when you are unable to close a dialogue box. Clicking on **OK** or **Cancel** removes the dialogue box temporarily: the dialogue box redisplays in a fraction of a second.

Until the bug is fixed, the workaround is to press the **<F2>** key, which displays the AutoCAD Text window and removes the dialogue box. ∎

Find File

▸ *First introduced in Release 12 for Windows*

Finding a DWG drawing file on today's large hard drives and local area networks can be a tough job—even if you do know the file's name. AutoLISP in Release 11 gained a findfile function that looks for files on the DOS and Acad paths.

In Release 12 for Windows, Autodesk turned the programming function into a user-friendly file searcher. Find File searches the current subdirectory or the entire hard drive or across connected network drives for DWG files or any filename you specify. Once Find File finishes searching, it presents a list of found files (see Figure). You load the file into AutoCAD by simply double-clicking on the name.

The **File** item on the menu bar lists the last four drawings you've loaded into AutoCAD. To load one of those drawings, simply single-click on its name.

▸ *How to access find file:*
```
File | Find File...
```

New Feature
Changed Function Keys

▶ *First introduced in Release 11 for Windows*

To make AutoCAD compatible with Windows, Autodesk has redefined four function keys, as follows:

Function Keys Changed in AutoCAD for Windows

Function Key	Windows Meaning	DOS Meaning
F1	Help	Flip screen
F2	Flip screen	Not used
F4	Tablet toggle	Not Used
F10	File menu	Tablet toggle

Two key changes, <F1> and <F10>, were made to make AutoCAD compatible with the Windows standard. The other two changes, <F2> and <F4>, accommodate the first two changes.

▶ *For more information on the Windows interface, see Chapter 2.*

New Feature
Context-sensitive Hyperlink Help

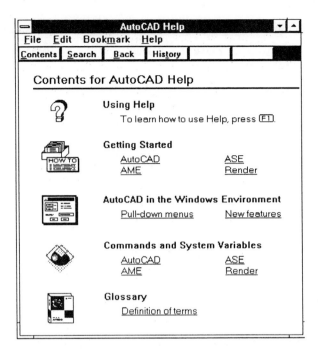

► *First introduced in Release 11 for Windows*

Release 11 for Windows digitized the entire AutoCAD *Reference Manual* as a single 11 MB file; the size was partly due to figures and tables being scanned in. While it was convenient to have the manual on-line, the size overwhelmed users who felt that much disk space wasn't worth giving up.

For Release 12, the on-line help (found in file AcadWin.Hlp) has been trimmed down to a mere 724 KB by providing information more concisely. Pressing the <F1> function key gives context-sensitive help during a command or pull-down menu; help is not available during dialogue boxes.

Terms underlined in green are linked to related topics; terms with a dashed green underline are linked to definitions. In either case, click on the green-underlined word to find out more.

► *How to access context-sensitive help:*
```
Help
```

New Feature
Independent Text Screen Window

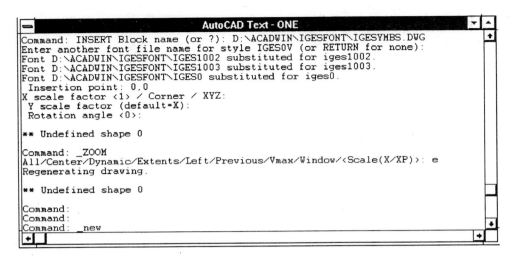

▶ *First introduced in Release 11 for Windows*

Under Windows, the AutoCAD text screen becomes an independent window with a useful logging function. You keep the text screen always displayed or bring it up for a brief look with the redefined <F2> function key. The text window is resizable and movable.

Instead of being limited to 25 lines as under DOS, the text screen lets you review up to 1,500 lines of command history via the scroll bar. The command history can be saved to a file on disk; unfortunately, the text screen has no copy-to-Clipboard function.

The **Preferences** dialogue box (accessed with the **File | Preferences...** command) lets you specify the size of command history (from 200 to 1,500 lines), whether a log file is kept and the name of the log file. The log file records everything in the text screen to a file on disk; this overcomes the 1,500-line limitation and the lack of Clipboard support.

▶ *How to access the text screen window:*
```
Edit | Text Window
```

On-the-fly Configuration

```
┌────────────────────── Preferences ──────────────────────┐
│ ┌─ AutoCAD Graphics Window ─┐  ┌─ AutoCAD Settings ─────┐ │
│ │  ☐ Screen Menu    ☐        │  │  ◉ Current Session     │ │
│ │  ☒ Toolbar    ☒ Toolbox    │  │  ○ AutoCAD Defaults    │ │
│ │  Command Prompt: [3 lines ▼]│  │  ○ Restore From ACAD.INI│ │
│ │  Window Repair:  [Bitmap  ▼]│  │  ○ Save To ACAD.INI    │ │
│ └────────────────────────────┘  └────────────────────────┘ │
│ ┌─ AutoCAD Text Window ──────┐  ┌─ Digitizer Input ──────┐ │
│ │  Number of scroll lines: [400]│ │  ◉ Digitizer Only      │ │
│ │  ☐ Log File Open           │  │  ○ Digitizer/Mouse Arbitrate│ │
│ └────────────────────────────┘  └────────────────────────┘ │
│  [  OK  ] [ Cancel ] [ Color... ] [ Fonts... ] [ Environment... ] [ Help... ] │
└──────────────────────────────────────────────────────────┘
```

- *First introduced in Release 11 for Windows*
- *Enhanced in Release 12 for Windows*

In earlier versions of AutoCAD, you exited the Drawing Editor to reconfigure AutoCAD. Changing the look of the Drawing Editor was limited to toggling the visibility of the status, menu, and command areas.

With Release 11 for Windows, AutoCAD allowed you to change the color and fonts used in the Drawing Editor and set the number of lines in the command prompt area from zero to three—without exiting the Drawing Editor. A feature useful to desktop publishing changes all drawing vectors to monochrome (black).

Release 12 enhances on-the-fly configuration to specify the environment variables that affect AutoCAD, AVE Render, and ASE; to toggle the visibility of scroll bars, toolbar and toolbox; and optionally to save the settings to the Acad.Ini file, an addition to the Acad.Cfg configuration file.

- *How to access on-the-fly configuration:*
  ```
  File | Preferences...
  ```

AVE Render

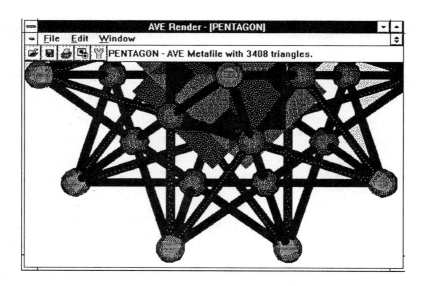

> ▸ *First introduced in Release 12 for DOS*
> ▸ *Enhanced in Release 12 for Windows*

Under Windows, the Render extension is (optionally) a stand-alone program. AVE Render displays to any 256- or 16.7 million graphics board supported by Windows; it prints to any graphics printer—monochrome or color—supported by Windows. AVE Render for Windows is MDI (multiple document interface) compliant. It displays more than one subwindow at a time to let you compare several renderings made by adjusting render parameters. AVE Render saves and reads renderings in WMF (Windows metafile) and BMP (bitmap) formats. AutoCAD drawings saved as a rendered WMF file can be imported back into AutoCAD. AVE Render can print the image on 130 A-size sheets to create a 100-inch printout, after gluing it together.

AVE Render requires 3 MB RAM beyond the 8 MB RAM for AutoCAD. Both the DOS and Windows versions of AVE Render lack RenderMan for creating photorealistic renderings.

> ▸ *How to access AVE Render:*
> Render | Render

> ▸ *For more information on AVE Render, see Chapter 11.*

ASVU

```
┌──────────────────────────────────────────────────────────────────────────┐
│ ▬        AutoCAD System Variables Utiltiy                                   │
├──────────────────────────────────────────────────────────────────────────┤
│ ⊠ More Info  [ Ok ]  [ Cancel ]  [ Refresh ]  [ Exit ]  Name: OSMode      │
│                                                                            │
│ ○ On ○ Off [←][  ]                       [→] Type: Integer Number          │
│                                                                            │
│ 2047  Qk & Nr & Tan & P & Ins & Int & Qd & Nd & Cnt & M & E               │
│ Sets object snap modes using the following bit-codes. To specify more than one │
│ osnap, enter the sum of their values. For example, entering 3 specifies the Endpoint │
│ (1) and Midpoint (2) osnaps.                                               │
│                                                                            │
│       0 = None.                                                            │
│       1 = Endpoint (E).                                                    │
│ ┌────────┐   Status: Read and Write      From: 0                           │
│ │ About  │   Saved to: Drawing           To: 2047                          │
│ └────────┘                                                                 │
└──────────────────────────────────────────────────────────────────────────┘
```

List box (right side): MenuCtl, MenuEcho, MenuName, MirrText, ModeMacro, OffsetDist, OrthoMode, OSMode, PDMode, PDSize, Perimeter, PFaceVMax, PickAdd, PickAuto

▸ *First introduced in Release 12 for Windows*

An undocumented feature, ASVU (AutoCAD system variable utility) lets you view the value and change the settings of AutoCAD's system variables. When you select a system variable from the list box (on the extreme right), the ASVU dialogue box displays all possible values. You can change the value by typing in a new value, by clicking the **On** and **Off** radio buttons or clicking on the scroll bar. When done, click on the **OK** button to update the value in AutoCAD.

ASVU is an example application written in Visual Basic v2. The source code is included in subdirectory \Acadwin\Vb\Asvu. You can improve the look of the dialogue box and change the programming code with Visual Basic.

▸ *How to access ASVU:*
1.   `Start AutoCAD`
2.   `Run \Acadwin\VB\Asvu\Asvu.Exe`

▸ *For more information on ASVU, see Chapter 14.*

New Feature
Multiple Sessions

Program Item Properties		
Description:	AcadWin FreePlot	OK
Command Line:	D:\ACADWIN\ACAD.EXE -p	Cancel
Working Directory:	d:\acadwin	
Shortcut Key:	None	Browse...
	☐ Run Minimized	Change Icon...
		Help

▶ *First introduced in Release 10 for OS/2*

When Autodesk came out with AutoCAD Release 10 for OS/2, it allowed you to run more than one session of AutoCAD at a time—as would be expected from an application in a multi-tasking operating system. When AutoCAD Release 11 for Windows was released, you could launch only one instance of the program. Users were disappointed.

In Release 12, you can run three copies of Release 12 at one time. With two AutoCADs running, you can exchange portions of drawings with each other. You can use one AutoCAD in freeplot mode to drive a plotter and printer; a second AutoCAD can be used for editing a drawing; the third AutoCAD could generate a hidden-line view or a rendering.

Two problems occur when running more than one AutoCAD at a time: four megabytes of RAM recommended for each additional copy of AutoCAD; running three AutoCADs with 1 MB drawings requires a computer with about 16 MB RAM. Since the computer has only one CPU, all copies of AutoCAD performing three tasks simultaneously are slower than performing them sequentially.

▶ *How to access multiple sessions:*
```
Double-click on the AutoCAD icon to start another
session of AutoCAD.
```

▶ *How to access freeplot mode:*
```
With the Program Manager, create a new icon with the
File | New... command (see Figure).
```

New Feature
Drag and Drop

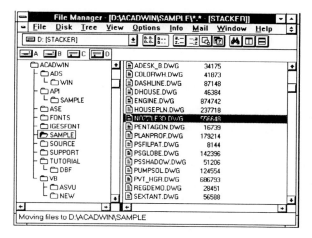

▸ *First introduced in Release 12 for Windows*

Windows v3.1 introduced *drag and drop*, which makes it easier to move words and cells, and load files into an application.

Release 12 for Windows implements drag and drop. When you drag an file icon onto the Drawing Editor graphics screen, AutoCAD loads the file. You can also drag a filename from the Windows File Manager.

Drag and drop lets you insert a text file into an AutoCAD drawing (the DText command must be started first) and lets you plot an AutoCAD drawing by dragging the DWG file onto the iconized Printer Manager.

▸ *For more information on drag and drop, see Chapter 6.*

Enhanced Feature
Windows Clipboard

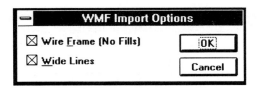

- *First introduced in Release 10 for OS/2*
- *Enhanced in Release 12 for Windows*

The Clipboard lets you move text and graphics between applications in a GUI operating environment. While the Clipboard supports any format of text or graphic, no applications program supports all possible formats.

For Release 12, Autodesk has greatly enhanced Clipboard support. Now you can copy AutoCAD drawings in WMF vector format or BMP raster format to the Clipboard. You can copy AutoCAD drawings in native DWG format (complete with extended entity data) between multiple AutoCAD sessions. You can paste ASCII text and WMF vector images into AutoCAD.

Even though Release 12 can import and display PCX, TIFF, and GIF raster images via a command-line interface, it cannot import BMP images via the Clipboard or any other way. You cannot copy text from the drawing to the Clipboard.

- *How to access the Clipboard:*
  All copy and paste functions are found in the Edit menu.

- *How to access the WMF paste options:*
  ```
  File | Import/Export > | WMF Import Options...
  ```

- *For more information on the Windows Clipboard, see Chapter 4.*

New Feature
Object Linking and Embedding

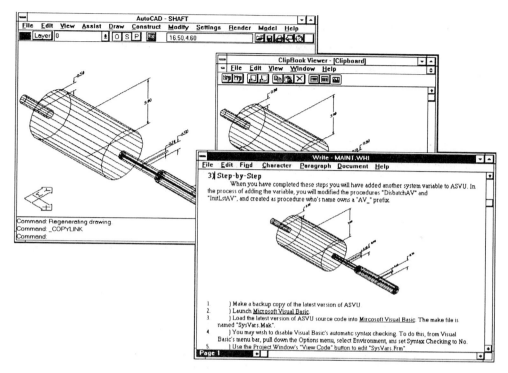

▶ *First Introduced in AutoSketch for Windows*

AutoCAD Release 12 for Windows mimics AutoSketch's ability to act as a Windows OLE server. That means you can link or embed an AutoCAD drawing in a Windows OLE client, such as Write and Cardfile.

When the drawing is *linked* to Write, it is automatically updated in Write when a change is made to the drawing. When a drawing is *embedded* in an OLE client, you manually update the link.

AutoCAD is not an OLE client, which means you cannot link or embed text, data, and graphics in AutoCAD from other OLE servers.

▶ *How to access object linking and embedding:*
```
Edit | Copy Link     or
Edit | Copy Embed
```

▶ *For more information on object linking and embedding, see Chapter 6.*

The Toolbar

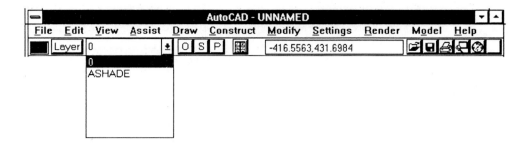

- *First introduced in Release 11 for Windows*
- *Enhanced in Release 12 for Windows*

Many Windows application boast a bar of buttons that make it easier to access frequently-used commands. In AutoCAD, you assign a single command, a script macro, or an AutoLISP routine to the button—on the fly! AutoCAD's implementation in Release 11 for Windows lets you display a predefined icon or a single character.

You define the meaning of a Toolbar button by clicking on the button with the right mouse button. The dialogue box lets you keep the meaning for just the current session or until it is changed again. As an enhancement in Release 12, Autodesk changed the precustomized buttons from object snap modes to toggle Toolbox, Open, Save, Zoom, Print, and Aerial View.

While you have a greater selection of icons to choose from in Release 12, you still cannot define your own icons as easily as in AutoSketch for Windows.

The Toolbar also displays the current color, layer name, and coordinates. It displays the settings of ortho, snap, and space modes. It gives direct access to several dialogue boxes and lets you easily change layers.

- *For more information on the Toolbar, see Chapter 12.*

New Feature
The Toolbox

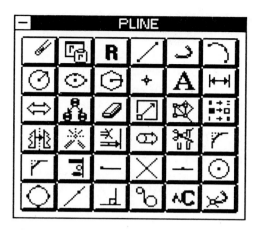

▶ *First introduced in AutoCAD Release 12 for Windows*

Along with display-list processing and bird's-eye view, third-party programmers came up with icon-based pop-up menus. These allow the user to quickly access a large number of AutoCAD commands and customized routines. However, these menus work only with specific graphics boards from certain vendors.

With Release 12 for Windows, Autodesk implemented the Toolbox as an icon menu that floats anywhere on the Windows desktop. The Toolbox is customized in the same manner as the Toolbar buttons; it comes predefined with 36 AutoCAD commands and macros. As you pass the cursor over the Toolbox's icons, the title bar displays the name of the icon's function.

Clicking on the Toolbox button on the Toolbar switches the Toolbox from being fixed to the left side of the Drawing Editor, to fixed on the right side, to floating free, to turned off.

▶ *How to access the Toolbox:*
`Click on the Toolbar's Toolbox icon.`

▶ *For more information on the Toolbox, see Chapter 12.*

Iconic Pop-down Menus

▸ *First introduced in Release 10 for Macintosh*

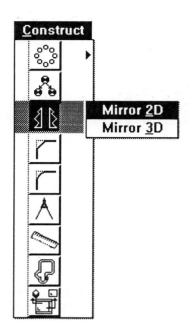

AutoCAD for Windows lets you substitute icons for words in the pop-down menus.

Most users recognize the function of a simple icon faster than a word label; icons are more international than a human language.

The drawback to an icon is that it takes time to learn its meaning.

AutoCAD for Windows lacks tear-off menus, as in AutoSketch for Windows or AutoCAD for the Macintosh.

You cannot create your own icons without purchasing an advanced programming language for Windows.

You fake having both an icon and a word for a menu item by duplicating the menu definition.

▸ *How to access iconic menus:*
```
Settings | Menu Bitmaps
```

Enhanced Feature
Macro Metacharacters, AutoLISP Functions, and ADS Commands

- *First introduced in Release 11 for Windows*
- *Enhanced in Release 12 for Windows*

AutoCAD for Windows uses the following ten metacharacters in menu macros:

Metacharacters Used by Release 12 for Windows

Char	Meaning
--	Separator line
->	Start child menu
<-	Terminate child menu
<-<-	Terminate parent menu
$(	Evaluate Diesel macro
~	Gray out menu item
!c	Prefix menu item with character c
!.	Prefix menu item with check mark
/	Specify accelerator key
^Xn^	Display icon Xn in place of text label

There are a number of new AutoLISP and ADS functions, most of which are for DDE (dynamic data exchange).

- *For more information on programming AutoCAD, see Section 4.*

New Feature
Dynamic Data Exchange

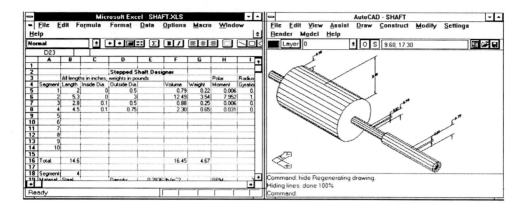

▸ *First introduced in Release 10 for OS/2*

DDE (short for dynamic data exchange) is the way OS/2 and Windows applications exchange data with each other. AutoCAD, Excel, 1-2-3, and WordPerfect are examples of applications that can exchange data via DDE. Not all Windows applications are DDE-aware.

AutoCAD Release 10 for OS/2 boasted a demo that used Microsoft Excel as the parametric engine that drove a shaft design in AutoCAD (see Figure). Change a value in the spreadsheet, and the AutoCAD drawing automatically updated. Use the Stretch command to change the shaft design, and the Excel spreadsheet automatically updated.

Since then, not much has changed except that AutoCAD Release 11 for Windows added support for Lotus 1-2-3.

▸ *How to access dynamic data exchange:*
Edit | DDE

▸ *For more information on dynamic data exchange, see Chapter 13.*

New Feature
Eight-Bit Text Translation

```
┌─────────────────────────────────────────────────────────┐
│                   DBTRANS Message                         │
├─────────────────────────────────────────────────────────┤
│ Updated system variable DWGCODEPAGE to "iso8859-1".       │
│                                                           │
│                                                           │
│                                                           │
│                      ┌──────────┐                         │
│                      │    OK    │                         │
│                      └──────────┘                         │
└─────────────────────────────────────────────────────────┘
```

▶ *First introduced in Release 12 for Windows*

While the first 128 ASCII characters are the same for all Roman languages, the remaining 127 change from language to language. The ASCII character set differs even between DOS and Windows. AutoCAD for DOS uses the character set defined by IBM for its Personal Computer, while AutoCAD for Windows uses the character set defined by ANSI.

DOS (and Windows) has the ability to change the character set by specifying a *code page*. Code pages have been defined for most European languages, including dialects such as American-English, Canadian-English, and French-Canadian.

Release 12 for Windows includes a new utility called "DbTrans" that corrects the display of eight-bit characters (over ASCII 128) in the drawing. That lets you edit a drawing created by an international version of AutoCAD. A second command, DDbTrans, is the dialogue box version of DbTrans.

▶ *How to access DbTrans:*
At the command prompt, type:
Command: **(xload "dbtrans")**
Command: **ddbtrans**

ODBC Support

```
┌──────────────────────────────────────────────────┐
│             Set Database Please Enter              │
│ ┌─Current Settings────────────────────────────────┐│
│ │  DBMS:   DBASE3                                  ││
│ │  Database: ASETUT                               ││
│ └─────────────────────────────────────────────────┘│
│  Username:  │                                       │
│  Password:  │                                       │
│                  ┌────────┐   ┌────────┐            │
│                  │   OK   │   │ Cancel │            │
│                  └────────┘   └────────┘            │
└──────────────────────────────────────────────────┘
```

▸ *First introduced in Release 12 for DOS*
▸ *Enhanced in Release 12 for Windows*

AutoCAD's database capabilities were greatly enhanced when Release 12 for DOS included support for SQL (structured query language) databases as an AME application called ASE (AutoCAD SQL extension). Release 12 for DOS and Windows includes drivers to link with Borland's dBase III+, dBase IV, and Paradox v3.5.

In the Windows world, there are two competing standards for linking applications with database programs. Borland developed IDAPI (integrated database application programming interface) while Microsoft has developed ODBC (open data base connectivity).

Release 12 for Windows includes the ODBC driver, which allows ASE to communicate with Windows database software, including Microsoft Access, Informix, and Oracle. AutoCAD does not include an IDAPI driver.

▸ *How to access AutoCAD's SQL extension:*
```
File | ASE
```

ADS Compiler Support

- *First introduced in Release 10 for OS/2*
- *Enhanced in Release 12 for Windows*

In Release 11 for Windows, Autodesk provided support for the Visual Basic programming environment via DDE. While the process worked, it didn't work well enough. Not a single commercial third-party application was written in Visual Basic 1 using the DDE link to AutoCAD.

If you don't write programs in Visual Basic, you can still run applications written by other programmers. Release 12 includes the VBRun200.Dll dynamic link library required to run Visual Basic apps.

The C and Basic compilers supported by AutoCAD Release 12 for Windows are:

- Borland C++ v3.0
- Metaware High C/C++ 3.0
- Microsoft C v6.0
- Microsoft C/C++ v7.0
- Microsoft QuickC for Windows
- Microsoft Visual Basic v2 Professional
- Watcom C/386 v9.0

- *For more information on programming with Visual Basic version 2, see Chapter 14.*

System Requirements

Autodesk recommends running AutoCAD Release 12 for Windows on a computer system with the following specifications:

    AutoCAD Release 12 for Windows
    Windows v3.1 running in enhanced mode on DOS v3.3 or higher

Plus one of the following systems:

▶ *Minimum system:*
    386 computer with math chip
    8 MB RAM
    8 MB hard disk space for minimum installation
    VGA graphics board and monitor
        (640 x 480 resolution and 16 colors)
    Two-button mouse
    Graphics printer

▶ *Recommended system:*
    486DX- or Pentium-based computer
    12 MB RAM plus 4 MB for each additional AutoCAD session
    33 MB hard disk space for full installation
    SuperVGA graphics board and monitor
        (1024 x 768 resolution and 256 colors, or better)
    Three-button mouse or digitizing tablet
    Laser printer or pen plotter

▶ *System recommended for this book:*
    Either of the above systems, plus:
    Windows-compatible sound board
    Microsoft Excel for Windows
    Visual Basic 2

Windows Navigation

Windows is an operating environment that can help you work more productively than under DOS. Windows is multitasking and allows interprocess communications. Multitasking means more than one program runs at a time; interprocess communications means the programs exchange data with each other without using files. Most important, Windows provides a uniform interface for all applications written to its standards. This chapter shows you how to navigate through Windows. If you know how to use one Windows program, you're on your way to using all others.

Executive Summary

When you learn one Windows application, you're well on your way to learning all other applications.

Starting Windows
- AutoCAD Release 12 for Windows requires DOS and Windows v3.1 or Windows for Workgroups in enhanced mode.
- Start Windows by type "Win" at the DOS prompt.

Anatomy of a Window
- AutoCAD and all Windows applications run in a window—either maximized to the full screen, in a window with a border, or minimized to an icon.
- Each window has a number of buttons to control the size and position of the window; other buttons control the view within the window.
- The title bar tells you the name of the application and data file; the menu bar gives you access to the application's commands.

Wrangling Rodents
- While you can use a keyboard with Windows, the mouse is much faster.
- Clicking the first button makes selections.
- Double-clicking executes programs or loads data files.
- Click and dragging selects more than one item or moves items.

The chapter concludes with a number of tips useful to running Windows more efficiently.

Starting Windows

You start Windows from the DOS prompt, as follows:

```
C:\> win
```

As Windows starts, it displays a logo screen (see Figure).

If you don't want to see the logo, add a space and a colon, as follows:

```
C:\> win :
```

You see a blank black screen until the Program Manager loads.

If you don't need to multitask DOS programs or need to run DOS

programs in a window, you can run Windows in *standard* mode. This mode runs Windows a bit faster and is the only way to run Windows if your computer has only 2 MB RAM. However, AutoCAD Release 12 for Windows runs only when Windows is in enhanced mode.

The Wimp Interface

The graphical user interfaces for today's desktop computers—such as Windows, OS/2, Macintosh, OSF/Motif, NextStep, and Solaris—employ the "WIMP" interface: *w*indows, *i*cons, *m*ouse, and *p*op-down menus.

Instead of seeing only one program on the computer screen at a time, you see more than one, each contained in its own window. Instead of remembering command names, you select from visual icons. Instead of typing in command names, you select commands with a mouse. Instead of pressing function keys and awkward <Ctrl>- and <Alt>-key combinations, you select from a pop-down menu.

In the following sections, you learn how to use the Wimp interface.

Anatomy of a Window

Everything in Windows runs in a window–hence the name. Each Window has several elements that control the size of the window, give information about the application, and let you control elements of the application (see Figure):

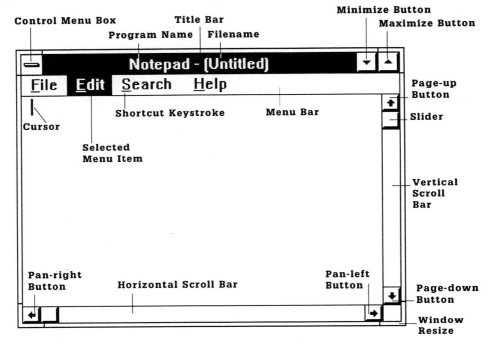

Control Menu Box | Title Bar | Minimize Button
Program Name | Filename | Maximize Button

Notepad - [Untitled]

File Edit Search Help

Cursor
Shortcut Keystroke Menu Bar
Selected Menu Item

Page-up Button
Slider

Vertical Scroll Bar

Pan-right Button | Horizontal Scroll Bar | Pan-left Button

Page-down Button
Window Resize

▶ **Control Menu Box** lets you do the minimize, maximize, size, and move functions with the keyboard. It also lets you switch to other programs.

▶ **Title Bar** lists the name of the application program, and the name of the file it is working with. If you haven't given the file a name yet, Windows calls the file "Untitled." You move a window by placing the cursor on the title bar, and holding down the mouse button. Drag the window to its new position, and let go of the mouse button.

▶ **Minimize and Maximize Buttons** change the size of the window to an icon (minimize) or to full-screen (maximize). To restore the program to its larger size, double-click on the icon. When the window is maximized, the maximize button turns into a double-ended arrow; clicking on the double-arrow restores the window to its smaller size.

▶ **Scroll Bars** pan drawings and documents too large to fit the window. There are two scroll bars—horizontal and vertical—but not all programs have both. You pan at three different speeds:

1. **Real-time pan.** Place the cursor on the slider, hold down the mouse button, and move the slider down or across. This is the fastest pan.

2. **Page pan.** Click on the scroll bar above and below the slider button. This pans the window one screenfull or page at a time.

3. **Slow pan.** Click on the buttons with arrows (such as the page-down button) to move one line at a time.

▶ **Window Resize** is controlled by the thin double-line border that surrounds the entire window. Resize by moving the cursor over the border (the cursor changes into a double-headed arrow), hold down the mouse button, and drag the window border to a new size. To move two sides of the window at once, grab one of the four corners of the window.

▶ **Menu Bar**, below the Title Bar, gives you access to the program's commands. Each item on the menu bar hides a pop-down menu. Select a menu item by moving the cursor over the item, then press the mouse button. The item turns black and a pop-down menu appears.

   Many applications have a several more bars below the menu bar: an icon bar (such as AutoCAD's Toolbar), and a ruler bar, commonly seen in word processing programs.

The Program Manager

When Windows is finished loading, it displays the Program Manager. This is not Windows; instead, the Program Manager is a *shell* that allows you to easily interact with Windows to start programs (see Figure).

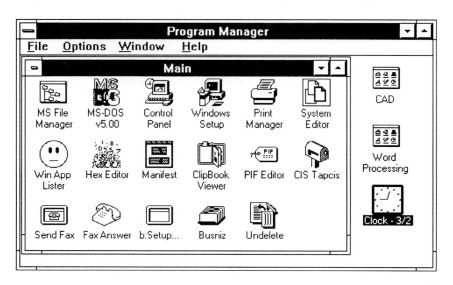

The Program Manager displays programs and files as *icons*. Each icon is labeled with a title to remind you of the icon's meaning. The Program Manager groups program icons into groups, called *program groups*. You can have one big group that holds all icons or a dozen groups that logically separate programs. For example, the Figure shows the Program Manager with one group called "Main," a group for CAD programs, and another for word processing.

The Program Manager supplied with Windows has some deficiencies. It does not integrate file management, and it does not let you place groups within groups. Consequently, you can replace Program Manager with third-party shells.

Wrangling Rodents

When the Macintosh was brand new, I took my fiancee to the first retailer in town displaying this new "computer for the rest of us." As we stood in front of the beaming Mac, I explained that she could control the computer by moving the mouse. My fiancee picked up the mouse and waved it in the air in front of the computer. "Nothing's happening," she puzzled.

Your ability to handle the mouse is key to your success with Windows. As an AutoCAD user, you have a legup on users new to Windows since you already use a mouse or digitizer. There are two aspects to rodent wrangling: (1) moving the on-screen cursor and (2) pressing the mouse buttons.

While Microsoft makes Windows and sells a mouse with two buttons, Windows only uses the left-hand button. A few Windows applications (including AutoCAD, to a limited extent) make use of the second right-hand button; none use the middle button of the three-button mouse.

So while Windows uses only one button of the two- and three-button mice, the button is used in four distinct ways:

1. **Click.** Press the mouse button once. This selects a menu item, places the text cursor, selects an AutoCAD Toolbar and Toolbox icon or selects a single graphical entity.

2. **Double-click.** Press the mouse button twice, quickly. This is the easiest and most common method to start a program: move the cursor over the program's icon, then double-click. Double clicking is also a short-cut in **File Open** dialogue boxes: double-click on the filename, instead of single-clicking on the file name then clicking on the **OK** button. Some software, such as WordPerfect, also makes use of triple and quadruple clicks.

3. **Click and drag.** Press the mouse button, hold the button down, move the mouse, and release the button. This highlights a section of text or makes a selection set of graphical entities in AutoCAD.

4. **<Shift>-click.** Sometimes additional functions are defined by pressing the mouse button while pressing a key on the keyboard. For example, pressing the **<Shift>** key in a program like AutoCAD adds to the selection set. Other key-mouse combinations include **<Ctrl>**-click, and **<Alt>**-click.

In emergencies when you have no access to the mouse, you can press the following keys on the keyboard:

▸ **<Alt>** moves the cursor to the menu bar.
▸ **<Tab>** moves between fields in a dialogue box.
▸ **<Enter>** confirms an action (the equivalent to a single click).
▸ **<Ctrl>-<Esc>** switches between programs.

Pop-down Menus

Pop-down menus in Windows are the same as those in AutoCAD for DOS. Autodesk borrowed the Release 12 for DOS interface from Windows, which borrowed from IBM's CUA (common user access) interface definition, which borrowed from the Apple Macintosh interface, which borrowed from research carried out by Xerox at its Palo Alto research center (see Figure). The pop-down menu has the elements you find in the AutoCAD for DOS menu:

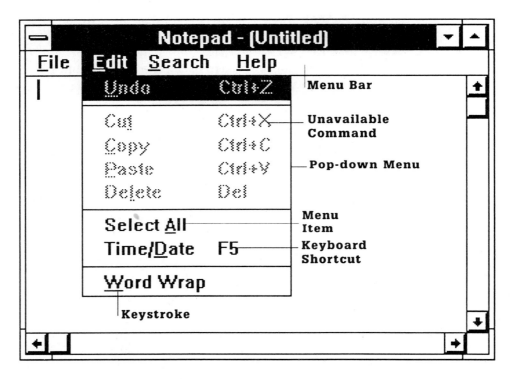

► Available commands are shown in black.

► Unavailable commands are shown in gray.

► The ellipsis (...) means the command displays a dialogue box.

► An arrow (►) means the command displays another pop-down menu, which is known by several names: a submenu, a child menu, and a cascading menu.

► A check mark (✓) in front of a command means it is turned on.

While Windows is meant to be used with a mouse, sometimes the mouse doesn't work or a keystroke is faster than moving the mouse around the screen. Pop-down menus have two kinds of keyboard shortcuts. Some commands have shortcut keys, such as F5 and **<Ctrl>-X** shown in the Figure. These directly get to the command without displaying the pop-down menu. To insert the time-date stamp, press **<F5>.**

All commands have the underlined character, such as <u>W</u> and <u>D</u> in the Figure. These are only available when the pop-down menu shows. To insert the time-date stamp, press **<Alt>** to access the menu bar, press E to get to the Edit menu, and press D to place the time-date stamp.

Dialoging with Boxes

When a command needs more information, it brings up a dialogue box. The dialogue box can simply ask you type something or it can have many elements:

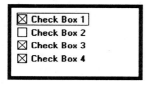

▶ **Check boxes** are square, and allow you to make one or more choices. An "X" appears when the option is turned on.

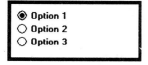

▶ **Radio buttons** are round or diamond and permit only a single choice. A dot appears when the option is selected.

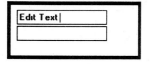

▶ **Text boxes** prompt you to enter text or numbers; use the delete, backspace, left- and right-arrow keys to edit the entry.

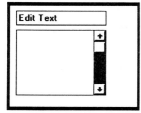

▶ **List boxes** display a list of choices. If the list is longer than the box, a scroll bar lets you see the rest of the list. Click to select an item.

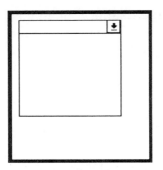

▶ **Drop-down list boxes** take up less screen real estate than the ordinary list box. Click on the down arrow to display the other choices. When you select an item by clicking on it, the list box disappears.

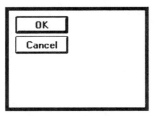

▶ **Buttons** provide ways to exit the dialogue box or bring up further dialogue boxes. The **OK** button exits the dialogue box and carries out the changes you made; the **Cancel** button exits without making changes; the **Help** button displays helpful information in another window.

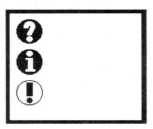

▶ **Special dialog boxes** display error and warning messages. The question mark (?) asks a question for clarification; the "**i**" presents an informative message; the exclamation mark (!) displays a warning; the stop sign displays an error (see Figure).

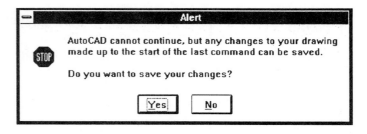

Eliminate Memory Conflicts

If you use QEMM-386, 386Max or another memory manager, you may need to tell the memory manager to exclude portions of high memory. For example, for the VMI DesignMaster VGA graphics board, QEMM-386 needs a parameter in Config.Sys such as "device=qemm386.Sys aram=a000-c7ff."

The ARAM statement tells QEMM not to use the memory area from a000 (in hexadecimal notation) to c7ff. After you install Windows, you need to add a similar statement to the System.Ini file, as follows:

```
[386Enh]
emmexclude=a000-c7ff
```

Using the NotePad text editor, search for the [386Enh] section and add the line "emmexclude= " with the memory range specified in the user's guide accompanying the graphics board. If the graphics board does not list a memory range to exclude, try running Windows without the EmmExclude statement; Windows takes into account the memory needs of ordinary VGA boards. It's the Super VGA and special purpose graphics boards using different areas of memory that cause problems. If you run into a problem, enter the range "a000-efff" for the EmmExclude statement, which covers the special needs of all add-in boards.

QEMM-386 v6 includes "stealth" technology, which makes memory available that is reserved for unused ROM chips. If Windows fails to load and you are using QEMM-386, check for the letters "ST:M" or "ST:F" in the following line located in the Config.Sys file:

```
device=c:\qemm386.sys ram st:m
```

Remove the offending characters, reboot the computer and try to load Windows. If successful and if you really need Stealth, ask Quarterdeck Office Systems for technical note #205, *Trouble-shooting Stealth*. ■

Double-click the Box

To close an application, or to exit Windows, double-click on the box (called the "Control Menu" box) in the extreme upper-left of the application's window. That's faster than selecting **File** and then picking **Exit**. ■

TIP NUMBER 5
Double-click the Title Bar

To maximize a window, double-click on the window's title bar. That's faster than picking the arrow button on the extreme upper-right corner of the window. ∎

TIP NUMBER 6
Windows within Windows

When you shell out to DOS from Windows for longer periods of time, you can forget that Windows is still loaded and running. You will, at least once in your life, type "Win" at the DOS prompt. The second copy of Windows gives you no warning that another copy is already running, unlike AutoCAD for DOS, which at least gives you the prompt C:\acad>> with the double arrow as a subtle reminder that you are shelled out from AutoCAD.

Create the same reminder as AutoCAD's as follows:

1. Create a batch file with the following two lines:

   ```
   prompt $p$g$g
   c:\command.com
   ```

   Save the batch file with the name Dos.Bat in the root (\) subdirectory. If you want a more blatant reminder, you can mimic WordPerfect's message, "Type EXIT to return to Windows. C:\>," as follows:

   ```
   prompt Type EXIT to return to Windows.$_$p$g
   c:\command.com
   ```

2. In the Program Manager, highlight the DOS Prompt icon by picking it once.

3. Press **<Alt>-<Enter>** to display the **Properties** dialogue box.

4. Change the Command Line from "Command.Com" to "C:\Dos.Bat" then pick the **OK** box. ∎

Windows Shortcut Keystrokes

Sometimes in Windows, it's faster to use the keyboard than the mouse. Here are the keyboard equivalents for some common operations:

- **<Alt>-FS**   Save file
- **<Alt>-FP**   Print or plot file
- **<Alt>-<Backspace>**   Undo previous action
- **<Shift>-<F4>**   Tile windows
- **<Shift>-<F5>**   Cascade windows
- **<Page Up>**   Move up by one screen
- **<Page Down>**   Move down by one screen
- **<Ctrl>-<Home>**   Move to top of file
- **<Ctrl>-<End>**   Move to bottom of file

Selecting a single file in the Windows File Manager is pretty easy. Selecting more than one file isn't. Here are the secrets to making multiple filename selections:

- Click-and-drag to select a group of files
- Or, click on the first filename, press the **<Shift>** key and click on the last filename
- Press **<Shift>-** (backslash) to select all files in the subdirectory
- Hold down the **<Ctrl>** key and click on filenames to select noncontiguous files
- Press **<Shift>-<F8>** for the selection cursor, which lets you select files by pressing the space bar ■

Increase Environment Space and Files

An error occurs if Windows has insufficient environment space and file handles. In the Config.Sys file, set the amount of environment space to a large number, such as 1024, and increase the number of file handles to 60, as follows:

```
shell=c:\dos\command.Com c:\dos\ /e:1024 /p
files=60                                      ■
```

Add More, More, More Memory

Windows thrives on RAM. The more memory your computer has, the more Windows uses. The more RAM Windows uses, the faster it runs.

- The 2 MB minimum amount recommended by Microsoft is a bad joke.
- The 8 MB recommended by Autodesk is fine for barely acceptable performance by AutoCAD for Windows. At this level, you'll experience disk thrashing as Windows moves programs and data in and out of RAM, to and from the swap file.
- From my experience, 12 MB is the minimum recommended.
- Add another 4MB if you use AVE rendering or AME solid modelling. ■

3

Display Processing

Release 12 for Windows is the first AutoCAD to include display-list processing, a cache that improves AutoCAD's redraw speed. The cache makes most zooms and pans much faster. Properly carried out, display-list processing also speeds up screen regeneration—albeit to a lesser extent. Autodesk has been criticized in comparative CAD reviews for AutoCAD's slow speed; AutoCAD Release 11 for Windows was not well received, in part for its painfully slow display speed. To cure both problems, Autodesk added a display-list processing graphics driver to Release 12. This chapter explains the technology and how to use the related Aerial View feature.

Executive Summary

Release 12 for Windows gives you four different options for its display drivers:

Display-List Processing

Pros:
- Redraws occur two times faster; zoomed-in pans occur 11 times faster
- Regenerations are 2% slower
- Aerial View feature is available

Cons:
- Display list consumes large amounts of valuable RAM
- Each viewport has its own display list
- Scroll bars are not available

GDI Bypass

Pros:
- Redraws occur 40% faster; zoomed-in pans occur 5% faster
- Regenerations occur 20% faster
- No additional RAM is consumed

Cons:
- Aerial View is not available; scroll bars are not available
- Screen cursor flickers noticeably

Combine Display-List Processing with GDI Bypass

Pros:
- Redraws occur five times faster; zoomed-in pans occur 13 times faster
- Regenerations occur 11% faster
- Aerial View is available

Cons:
- Significant memory requirement
- Screen cursor flickers noticeably
- Scroll bars not available

Disable Display-List Processing and GDI Bypass

Pros:
- More memory is available; scroll bars are available
- Screen cursor does not flicker

Cons:
- Slower redraws, regens, and zoomed-in pans
- Aerial View is not available

Turn on display-list processing (unless you find AutoCAD spends a lot of its time paging to disk); turn off GDI-bypass to avoid cursor flicker.

What Is Display-List Processing?

AutoCAD stores entities in a drawing with 64-bit double-precision real numbers. To display the drawing on the screen, AutoCAD doesn't need to be that accurate. The screen display is relatively crude at about 75 dpi (dots per inch), an accuracy of just two significant places.

From version 2.5 until Release 11, AutoCAD converted the 64-bit real-number database into a list of 15-bit integer entities, which are displayed on the screen. The list of displayed entities is called the "display list." The conversion of the database to display list is called "regeneration." (Prior to version 2.5, AutoCAD rebuilt the display list with every zoom and pan.)

When you do a small zoom, such as Zoom 5, the view redraws quickly. AutoCAD is using the display list to update the screen view—this is called a "redraw." When you zoom in deep, such as Zoom 200, the new view appears more slowly—this is called an "accidental" regen. The limit of the integer-based display list is reached and AutoCAD rebuilds the display list, causing the regeneration.

There are a number of situations when display-list processing is unable to improve the display speed. AutoCAD's display in paper space, the text screen, the Hide command's hidden-line removal, the Dview command's perspective mode, and the Shade and Render commands' renderings can be sped up only with a faster CPU or improved algorithms.

Back in 1985, the venerable Nozzle.Dwg drawing took 270 seconds (nearly 5 minutes) to redraw with each zoom or pan, using a mathchipless XT. Today, with ever faster CPUs coupled to display-list processing, the zoom and pan times take as long as it takes to press the <Enter> key—about 0.03 seconds, a 9,000-fold increase in speed.

Integrated Display-List Processing

Autodesk made two display-speed improvements to AutoCAD Release 12 for Windows: (1) regenerations occur less frequently; (2) redraws are faster. Let's take a look at how Autodesk programmers accomplished this.

Less Frequent Regens. Regenerations occur less frequently with Release 12 because Autodesk increased the size of the display list. Previous to Release 12, AutoCAD used a 15-bit display list, which allowed a VGA-resolution graphics board to zoom in 50 times before needing to rebuild the display list. Release 12 doubled the size of the integer to 31 bits (yes, *31* bits and not the 32 bits advertised by Autodesk). That's a 2,097,152:1 zoom ratio—the equivalent of zooming a view of size of the Earth's diameter down to 20 feet. All operating system versions of Release 12 have the 31-bit display list.

Faster Redraws. Redraws are faster because Release 12 for Windows includes an Autodesk-written display driver that speeds up the sluggish performance under Windows. The display driver, called the Windows Accelerated driver, does this by two means: (1) display-list processing and (2) bypassing the Windows GDI (graphical display interface). The advantages to display-list processing are:

- **Redraws** are twice as fast.
- **Zoomed-in pans** are 11 times faster.
- **Regenerations** are 2% slower.

Combining display-list processing with bypassing the GDI gives the additional speed advantages:

- **Redraws** are five times faster.
- **Zoomed-in pans** are 13 times faster.
- **Regenerations** are 11% faster.

To test the benefit of Autodesk's accelerated Windows driver, I benchmarked Release 12 with the HousePln.Dwg drawing file (found in subdirectory \AcadWin\Sample) at 640 x 480 resolution. The results are shown in the Table below:

Benchmarking AutoCAD Windows

Display Driver	Redraw Time	Regen Time	Pan Time	Memory Consumption
Windows Accelerated Driver				
DLP and GDI Bypass enabled	3.4 sec	28.1 sec	0.4 sec	7.2 MB
GDI Bypass disabled	7.6 sec	32.1 sec	0.5 sec	7.2 MB
DLP disabled	11.4 sec	26.1 sec	5.0 sec	6.6 MB
DLP and GDI bypass disabled	16.7 sec	31.4 sec	5.5 sec	6.6 MB
Windows Plain Driver	16.7 sec	31.5 sec	0.7 sec	6.4 MB

From the results, note that Autodesk's display-list processing code is only partially effective at speeding up AutoCAD's display speed; the display-list processor has its greatest effect on zoomed-in panning. A great deal of the speed increase with the Redraw and Regen commands comes from bypassing the GDI.

The Cost of Speed. All this new speed comes at a cost. The display-list caching and 31-bit display list use up megabytes of memory with even medium-size drawings. From the table, note that the display list takes up 600 KB (7.2 MB - 6.6 MB = 0.6 MB) of memory to hold a drawing with a file size of only 240 KB!

When you work with more than one viewport, AutoCAD creates a display list for each viewport. Opening four viewports creates four display lists that consume 2.8 MB of memory—11 times the size of the size of the DWG file. The undocumented command **DsDrv_Stat** displays a dialogue box summarizing the memory consumption (see Figure).

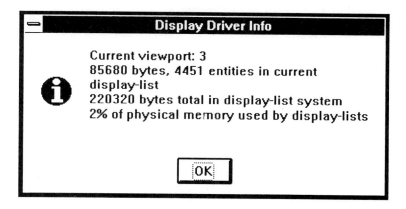

The dialogue box indicates that the current viewport (3) uses 85 KB of memory to store the display list. All of the viewports use 220 KB of memory. If your computer system is running short of memory, you can disable the display-list processing with the undocumented **DsDrv_Config** command.

The second greatest consumer of RAM is Release 12's 31-bit display list. Doubling the width of the integer doubles, triples, and quadruples the size of the display list, depending on how the driver was written. While the Autodesk-written driver does not allow user to reduce the display list from 31 bits to 15 bits, third-party drivers from Artist Graphics and Vermont Microsystems do. Unless you really want the millionfold zoom, I recommend you select the 15-bit display list with a third-party driver.

Ironically, due to the memory consumption of these speed enhancing features, AutoCAD runs slower when its memory demands exceed the amount of available RAM. Running AutoCAD Release 12 for Windows with display-list processing consumes nearly 14 MB of memory with four viewports open on the 240 KB HousePln drawing.

In addition, there are a number of minor catches to Release 12's gee-whiz features. The 31-bit display list permits a two million zoom ratio but only in theory. In practice, AutoCAD is limited to a maximum regen-free zoom of 769,362:1 from an initial regeneration. The Zoom Vmax is now much larger than the Zoom Extents to allow zooming out; hence, the practical regen-free zoom ratio is one-third the theoretical ratio.

While the GDI bypass feature consumes no RAM, it does create two irritants. The most apparent is when you experience cursor flicker of both the AutoCAD crosshair and the Windows cursor. The Windows cursor flickers everywhere on the desktop whenever AutoCAD is running.

The GDI normally controls everything that appears on your computer's screen, including what happens when one window overlaps another window. Since it bypasses the GDI, AutoCAD's driver has to maintain the desktop presentation space and perform all clipping on its own. Otherwise, you have problems of overlapping windows that aren't cleaned up properly.

The Feature List

The features in a display-list driver, whether from Autodesk or from a third-party, differ between drivers. The following sections describe features found in Autodesk and third-party drivers.

Price. While Release 12 for Windows includes free display-list processing and some additional features, you may want to try a third-party product. Before buying, though, get a demo disk from the vendor to try out the features and user interface.

Other Software. Third-party packages include a separate driver for AVE Render, AutoShade, RenderMan, and 3D Studio to provide high-color, high-resolution images. AutoCAD for Windows includes a Windows driver for AVE Render. None benefit from display-list processing.

Bird's-Eye View. The *bird's-eye view* is a small window that displays the equivalent of a Zoom-Extents view of the drawing (see Figure). As you zoom and pan about the drawing, the bird's-eye view moves a rectangle that represents the current view. Autodesk calls its bird's-eye view the "Aerial View," which floats anywhere on the Windows desktop.

Notice in the figure how the Aerial View shows the entire drawing, while AutoCAD shows a closeup of two desks.

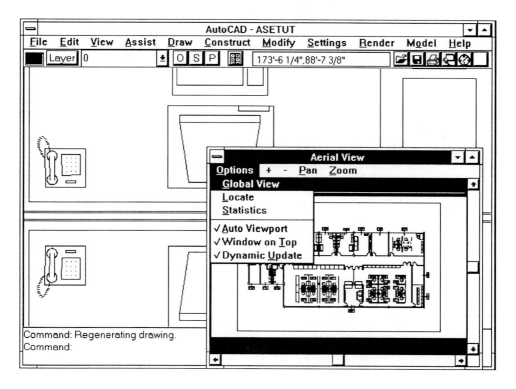

Spyglass. As you move the cursor around the drawing, the *spyglass* window shows the magnified view under the cursor (see Figure). Autodesk's Aerial View works as either a bird's-eye view or a spyglass but not both. I suggest you set ViewRes to 20,000 so that circles don't look like octagons under the spyglass. In the figure, notice how the Aerial View shows a closeup of two desks, while AutoCAD shows the entire drawing.

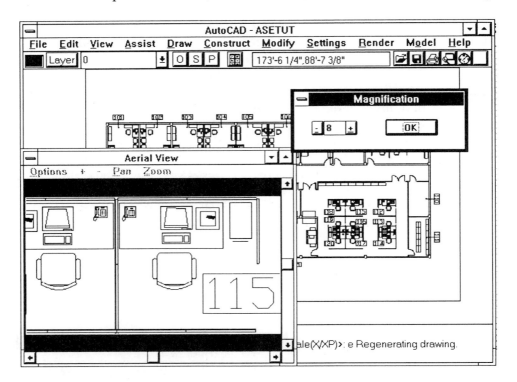

Dynamic Pan and Zoom. Display-list processing drivers are fast enough that they can provide you with *dynamic panning and zooming.* Here the view pans and zooms in realtime as you move the cursor within the bird's-eye view. Aerial View provides dynamic panning in spyglass mode.

Edge Panning. *Edge panning* is a variation on dynamic panning; the view pans when the cursor pauses at the edge of the graphics screen. You may not care for the drawing sliding around the screen on its own!

Drawing Viewer. Third-party display driver sometimes include a built-in drawing viewer. This lets you view another drawing without consuming as much RAM as loading a second copy of AutoCAD. AutoCAD does not include a DWG file viewer.

15-/31-bit Display List. The 31-bit display list significantly increases the size of the display-list. Third-party display drivers have the option of reducing the display list to 15 bits.

Digitizer Buttons. AutoCAD lets you define up to 15 digitizer buttons. Third-party display drivers let you define the buttons without needing to rewrite the Acad.Mnu file and double, triple and quadruple the number of button functions by letting you define the meaning of double-click, **<Shift>**-click, and long-click combinations.

Anti-aliasing. By applying *anti-aliasing* to nonorthogonal vectors, AutoCAD's curved and diagonal lines look perfectly smooth (see Figures), increasing the apparent resolution. The drawback is that software anti-aliasing slows down the display speed (due to the added processing overhead) and reduces the displayable colors from 256 to 16. In a drawing with many diagonal lines, the redraw speed is twice as slow as in a drawing with mostly orthogonal lines.

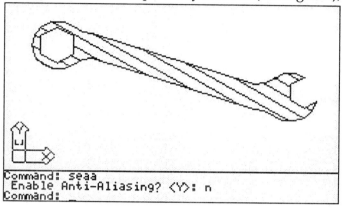

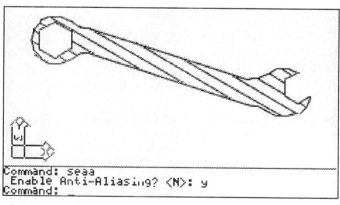

Hardware Lock. International versions of AutoCAD and some third-party display drivers use a hardware lock that attaches to the parallel port.

Whether the features are useful—or even necessary—depends on how you work with AutoCAD. Try them all out and check if you find send yourself still using them after a month. If not, you don't need the feature.

The Aerial View

The Aerial View feature (new in Release 12 for Windows) implements bird's-eye view and spyglass features for AutoCAD. To turn on Aerial View, click on the Aerial View icon on the Toolbar or type, as follows:

```
Command: dsviewer
```

The bird's-eye view acts as a map to the drawing. It shows the equivalent to the Zoom-Extents view; an inset rectangle indicates the current view. You can think of Aerial View as a Windows-style replacement for the Zoom Dynamic screen.

The Aerial View can switch to a spyglass mode. The spyglass performs the opposite function to the bird's-eye view. As you move the cursor around, the spyglass displays a zoomed-in view under the cursor. You can adjust the spyglass magnification from 2x to 32x of the current view.

Autodesk easily implemented the Aerial View because it is a function that depends on display-list processing. Since the Windows Accelerated display driver stores the entire drawing in a special display list, it is fairly trivial to provide the bird's-eye view and spyglass features. Turning on Aerial View consumes no additional RAM.

You will find that Aerial View gets in the way on low-resolution displays, such as VGA (640 x 480). You should run AutoCAD at 800 x 600 resolution at the least. There are three special cases to using Aerial View: three-dimensional drawings, multiple viewports and spyglass mode.

3D Drawings

When you work with a 3D drawing, the Aerial View displays the Zoom-Extents view of the current viewpoint in three dimensions. However, Aerial View has the unfortunate characteristic of being unfriendly to most modes of three-dimensional drafting. As long as the drawing is displayed as an orthogonal wireframe, Aerial View works fine.

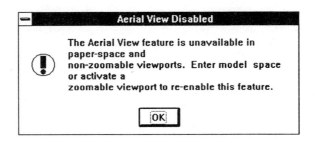

When you invoke the Hide, Shade, or Dview Zoom commands, then the Aerial View window disappears. When you try to bring Aerial View back, AutoCAD warns "The Aerial View feature is unavailable in paper-space and non-zoomable viewports" (see Figure).

Neither the on-line help nor the printed documentation explains that a "non-zoomable viewport" is a viewport in perspective mode, or has hidden lines removed, or has been shaded. You remove perspective mode with the **Plan** command; you remove hidden-line and shaded views with the **Regen** command.

Multiple Viewports. When you work with more than one viewport, Aerial View displays the Zoom Extents of the current viewport—the viewport you are currently working in (see Figure, next page). You will notice that the image in the Aerial View matches the shape of the viewport.

If you work with more than one copy of AutoCAD, you can bring up an Aerial View window for each. To help you keep track of which Aerial View window belongs to which AutoCAD, the title bar changes to "Aerial View - 1." Aerial View does not work when AutoCAD is started in freeplot mode.

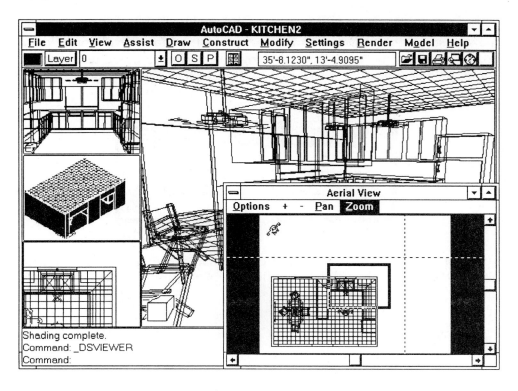

Spyglass Mode. The spyglass mode is an excellent way to inspect details of a drawing without repeated zoom-ins and -outs. Inside the Aerial View window, AutoCAD dynamically pans the view as you move the cursor around the drawing.

To access spyglass mode, select **Options | Locate** from the Aerial View menu bar. The full-screen crosshair cursor changes to a short crosshair cursor. As you move the cursor around the drawing, the Aerial View displays a zoomed-in view under the cursor.

By default, the zoom ratio is 8x. You change the zoom ratio by clicking the mouse's right button. AutoCAD displays the **Magnification** dialogue box (see Figure). By repeatedly clicking on the - button, you decrease the zoom ratio down to 2x; click the + button to increase the zoom ratio to 32x. Click the **OK** button to dismiss the dialogue box.

Spyglass mode does not work in "non-zoomable" viewports, as described above. When working with multiple viewports, you cannot pan over to another viewport.

Aerial View Not Available.

Sometimes the Aerial View does not work due to the following reasons:

▸ AutoCAD is not configured with the Windows Accelerated display driver. Use the **Config** command to reconfigure the video display.

▸ The display-list processing option is not turned on. Use the **DsDrv_Config** command to turn on the option.

▸ If the computer system does not have enough free memory, AutoCAD does not allow display-list processing and, consequently, Aerial View.

▸ AutoCAD is in paper space. Switch to model space with **MSpace** command.

▸ A viewport is displaying perspective mode or a view with hidden lines removed or a shaded view. Autodesk calls each of these "a non-zoomable viewport." Turn off the perspective mode with the **Plan** command; remove the hidden lines and shading with the **Regen** command.

▸ AutoCAD is in freeplot mode. In this case, the plot preview display works as a substitute for the Aerial View window. ▪

Aerial View Shortcuts

Aerial View has four shortcuts to make it easier to use:

▸ Click on the - and + items on the menu bar. That quickly decreases and increases the zoom level of the Aerial View in increments of two.

▸ Double-click on the **Zoom** item on the menu bar. That makes the viewport match the zoom level in the Aerial View window.

▸ Click the title bar of the Aerial View. That updates the Aerial View to match the current viewport when **Auto Viewport** is toggled off.

▸ Click on the scroll bars. That lets you pan while in Zoom mode. ▪

New Commands

Release 12 for Windows adds new commands to AutoCAD for controlling the Aerial View. Four commands work at the Command: prompt; they can be used in menu macros and AutoLISP routines. The other commands are only available by making menu selections in the Aerial View window. The commands are summarized by the Table, below.

Summary of Aerial View Commands

Command	Aerial View Menu Picks	Meaning
DsViewer	...	Turns on Aerial View
DsViewer_Off	...	Turns off Aerial View
DsDrv_Config	...	Dialogue box toggles display-list processing and GDI bypass
DsDrv_Stat	Options | Statistics	Dialogue box displays display list statistics
...	Options | Global View	Displays Zoom-Extents view of drawing
...	Options | Locate	Switches Aerial View to spyglass mode
...	Options | Auto Viewport	Toggles whether Aerial View automatically displays current viewport
...	Options | Window on Top	Toggles whether Aerial View floats on top of AutoCAD
...	Options | Dynamic Update	Toggles real-time updates of Aerial View during editing
...	+	Increases magnification
...	-	Reduces magnification
...	Pan	Lets you pan at the current zoom ratio
...	Zoom	Lets you zoom into the view

Integrating AutoCAD

The Windows Clipboard

Proprietary file formats have long dogged users in the DOS world. You know the problem: you can't bring an AutoCAD DWG file into WordPerfect as a graphic without first translating it to another graphics format, such as DXF, SLD or HPGL; AutoCAD can't import text from a WordPerfect document without first translating it to ASCII text format. This chapter describes how the Windows Clipboard solves some of the problems of exchanging data between applications.

Executive Summary

AutoCAD for Windows has six commands that interact with the Windows Clipboard. This chapter describes four of the six commands: **CopyImage**, **CopyClip**, **PasteClip**, and the **Edit | Paste Command** menu selection. The commands are used as follows:

CopyImage
- ▶ Menu selection: **Edit | Copy Image**
- ▶ Copies the AutoCAD image in BMP bitmap (raster) format
- ▶ Captures most of the AutoCAD screen to the Clipboard: the Toolbar, the drawing area, the sidebar menu, the Command prompt area, as well as the floating Toolbox and Aerial View
- ▶ AutoCAD cannot paste BMP raster images from the Clipboard into a drawing
- ▶ AutoCAD exports the raster image to a file on disk in DIB (device-independent bitmap) with the **SaveDib** command (menu pick: **File | Save DIB**)

CopyClip
- ▶ Menu selection: **Edit | Copy Vectors**
- ▶ Copies the AutoCAD image in WMF Windows metafile (vector) format
- ▶ Captures only drawing entities to the Clipboard
- ▶ AutoCAD pastes WMF vector images from the Clipboard into a drawing with the **PasteClip** command

PasteClip
- ▶ Menu selection: **Edit | Paste**
- ▶ Pastes WMF images from the Clipboard into an AutoCAD drawing
- ▶ WMF image is inserted as a block (made of polylines) with the generic name WMF*n*
- ▶ The **WMFopts** command controls how the WMF image is converted to AutoCAD format: with or without filled wide lines and filled areas (menu pick: **File | Import/Export | WMF In Options...**)
- ▶ AutoCAD imports a WMF file from disk with the **WMFin** command (menu pick: **File | Import/Export | WMF In...**)

Paste Command
- ▶ Menu selection: **Edit | Paste Command**
- ▶ Pastes plain ASCII text from the Clipboard into an AutoCAD drawing
- ▶ Before pasting text, you must start the **DText** command
- ▶ AutoCAD does not convert text attributes, such as tabs, boldface and italic
- ▶ AutoCAD cannot export text to the Clipboard

Any Flavor You Like

Standard file formats (such as DXF for CAD drawings and ASCII for text) ease the obstacle to productivity. But standards have proliferated, making it difficult for a software house to support all standards.

For example, AutoCAD exports drawings in two dozen formats: ASCII and binary ADI (Autodesk Device Interface), ASCII and binary DXF (Drawing eXchange Format), ASM (AutoSolid Model), BMP (Windows bitmap), DIB (Windows Device-Independent Bitmap), DM/PL (Digital Microprocessor/Plotter Language), DWG (DraWinG), DXB (Drawing eXchange Binary), FLM (FiLMroll), GIF (CompuServe Graphics Interchange Format), HPGL and HPGL/2 (Hewlett-Packard Graphics Language), IGES (Initial Graphics Exchange Specification), PCL (Printer Control Language), PCX (PC Paintbrush), PS (PostScript), SLD (SLiDe), STL (STereoLithography), TIFF (tagged image file format), WMF (Windows MetaFile), and more.

WordPerfect imports graphic images, either directly or via the GraphCnv conversion program, in even more formats: ASCII DXF (Drawing eXchange Format), BMP (BitMaP), CGM (Computer Graphics Metafile), DHP (Dr. Halo PIC), EPS (Encapsulated PostScript), GEM (Graphical Environment Manager), HPGL (Hewlett-Packard Graphics Language), IMG (IMaGe), MSP (MicroSoft Paint), PCX (PC paintbrush), PIC (PICture), PNTG (PaiNTinG), PPIC (Pc plus PICture), TIFF (Tagged Image File Format), WMF (Windows MetaFile), and WPG (WordPerfect Graphics).

In spite of these two long lists, neither program supports all the "standards" in common. Despite the alphabet soup of abbreviations, only a few formats are in common between AutoCAD and WordPerfect.

Even when two programs appear to share a file format, the standard is not fully implemented. For example, WordPerfect does not import portions of a DXF file that involved oblique text, special text characters, and fitted polylines. Even if you find a file format that works accurately in one direction, it may not work in the other direction. For example, AutoCAD produces HPGL and HPGL/2 files but cannot read them.

The Windows Clipboard

Microsoft Windows partially solves these problems with the Clipboard. It makes data exchange more transparent and it reduces the number of standards.

When you use the **Cut** and **Copy** commands in a Windows application, you cut and copy to the Windows Clipboard—perhaps without knowing it. This is different from DOS-based programs, where you cut or copy to a memory buffer reserved by the program itself. Since the cut or copied piece is stored in the Clipboard, the piece can be used by the same application or by almost any other Windows application.

When you use the **Paste** command to insert the copied piece, you paste from the Clipboard. After pasting into the application, a copy remains in the Clipboard. That lets you paste the same piece more than once.

The Clipboard is a temporary storage place. Its contents are erased the next time you use the **Copy** or **Cut** command. To save the contents of the Clipboard, follow one of these options:

- ▶ Use the **Paste** command to insert the contents into an application

- ▶ Some programs have an **Append** command that lets you add text to the text already in the Clipboard

- ▶ Use the Clipboard program's **File | Save As...** command to save the contents of the Clipboard as a CLP file on disk

- ▶ If your computer uses Windows for Workgroups, you save more than one clipping in the Clipbook Viewer (see Figure)

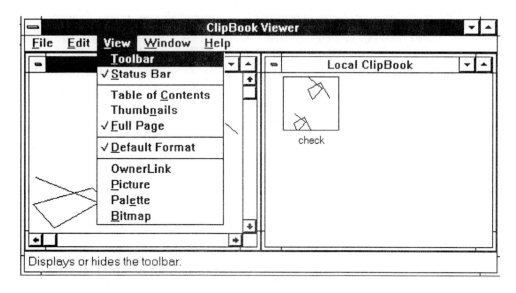

Since text and graphics are moved and copied from one application to another, the Clipboard becomes a powerful form of data transfer without the need to use files on disk.

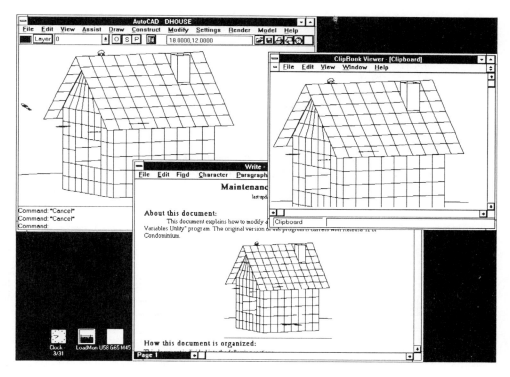

The Figure above shows a drawing created in AutoCAD (top) copied to the Clipboard (center right), pasted into a Write document as a graphic (bottom). Once the image is in another program, you move and resize the picture to fit your needs.

Using the Clipboard with AutoCAD

AutoCAD for Windows supports most—but not all—of the Clipboard's capabilities. You can copy graphics from the drawing in raster or vector form; paste vector graphics and text into the drawing. You cannot copy text from the drawing, nor can you paste raster graphics into the drawing.

These capabilities let you easily bring an AutoCAD drawing into a desktop publishing package, import a detail drawing from another CAD package, and insert text in an AutoCAD drawing from a text editor. Unfortunately, you cannot export text via the Clipboard for spell checking with Release 12 for Windows. The workaround continues to be the DXFout Entities command or to use a third-party spell checker that works inside of AutoCAD.

AutoCAD's Clipboard-related commands are located in the **Edit** menu (see Figure):

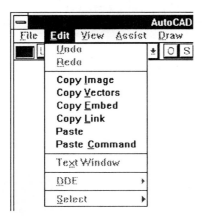

Copy Image (CopyImage command) prompts you to select a rectangular area of the AutoCAD screen. You can copy the drawing area, the Toolbar, side screen area, and the command area (see Figure). If the Toolbar and Aerial View are floating over the AutoCAD window, they are also copied. The area you select is copied to the Clipboard in bitmap format.

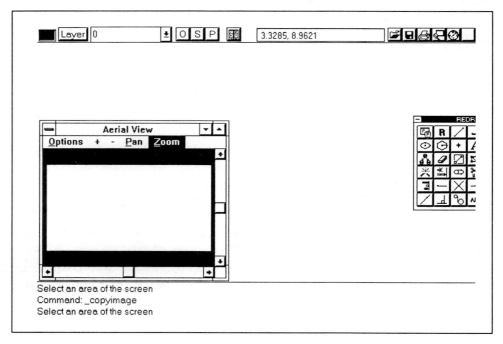

Copy Vectors (CopyClip command) prompts you to select a portion of the AutoCAD drawing. The entities you select are copied to the Clipboard in AutoCAD and WMF (Windows metafile) format, called "picture" by the Clipboard.

Copy Embed (CopyEmbed command) copies vector/raster to the Clipboard in native, ownerlink, and picture formats. The drawing can then be embedded in another Windows application that acts as an OLE client (see Chapter 6, "Object Linking and Embedding").

Copy Link (CopyLink command) copies vector/raster to the Clipboard in ownerlink, picture, bitmap, and palette formats. The drawing can then be linked to another Windows application that acts as an OLE client.

Paste (PasteClip command) pastes WMF vector images into the drawing as a block named WMFn. The **File | Import/Export | Wmf In Options..** (WmfOpts) command lets you toggle two import features: (1) whether solid areas are displayed and (2) whether wide lines are displayed.

Paste Command inserts text into the drawing from the Clipboard after the **DText** (or **Text**) command has started. In Release 11, the command is called "Paste Text."

Print Screen In addition to AutoCAD's Clipboard commands, copies the entire screen to the Clipboard when you press the **<Print Screen>** key, or you can press the **<Alt><Print Screen>** key to copy just the topmost window, such as a dialogue box.

With the Clipboard's **Display** menu, you can toggle between DIB (device-independent bitmap) format or BMP bitmap format.
You cannot *cut* a graphic out of AutoCAD; only copying is allowed.
    You cannot paste BMP bitmap raster images into AutoCAD with the **Edit | Paste** command. Instead, use the **GifIn**, **PcxIn**, and **TiffIn** commands to import a raster image in one of the three formats.
    In Release 12, AutoCAD dropped the Release 11 **Edit | Start Clipboard** command, which brought the Clipboard to the top of the desktop.

Raster or Vector?

AutoCAD for Windows lets you copy an image of the drawing to the Windows Clipboard in two formats : raster and vector.

The raster format is an accurate copy of what appears on the screen. If you use a low resolution screen, such as 640 x 480 VGA, you get an accurate copy of that low-resolution image (see Figure).

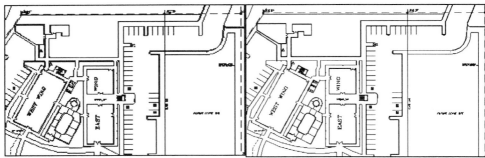

Raster at 640 x 480 resolution...   *...and at 1024 x 768 resolution.*

The **CopyImage** command lets you make a raster copy of any AutoCAD screen, whether 2D, 3D, multiple viewports, shade, with hidden lines removed, or a slide. The raster copy lets you clip a clean rectangle of a detail, which the vector copy can't.

The raster format has two drawbacks. The BMP format takes up a lot of disk space—130 KB for a VGA resolution 16-color image; 730 KB for a 1024 x 768-resolution, 256-color image. You lose individual entities as each is converted to a pattern of dots.

The vector format takes up far less disk space, typically 30 KB. You can't copy, in vector format, AutoCAD images made with the Shade or Vslide commands (since they are raster representations) or across several viewports. But you can capture a hidden line view in vector form; however, the 3D information is lost. You cannot clip a clean rectangle out of the image but you can select individual entities. The resolution of vector-based images is not dependent on the resolution of the graphics screen: the printed output looks smoother. Changing the scale of the vector image doesn't loose resolution. Since you are dealing with vectors, you can select specific entities to copy.

Before deciding between copying the drawing in raster or vector, think about the ultimate destination. The destination may be limited to either raster (BMP) or vector (WMF) format. If both choices are available, then choose BMP if you want to represent AutoCAD and choose WMF if you want to represent the drawing.

Tutorial 1
Copying Bitmaps from AutoCAD

In this first Clipboard tutorial, we copy a raster image from AutoCAD and insert it in the Windows Write word processor, which is included with every copy of Windows.

1. Load AutoCAD and open the Sample.Dwg file, found in subdirectory \Acadwin\Sample.

2. The **Copy Image** command asks you specify a windowed area. To copy the full-screen image, it helps to zoom out a bit, as follows:

```
Command: zoom e
Command: zoom 0.95x
```

   The two commands place a small blank area around the drawing. If, instead, you want to copy a detail, the resolution is improved when you use the Zoom W command to enlarge the detail.

3. If you are working with a black-and-white document, you get better results by changing all colors to black. Select **File | Preferences...**, pick the **Colors...** button, then check the **Monochrome vectors** box. Click on the **OK** button, twice.

4. Pick **Edit** from the menu bar, then select the **Copy Image** command. A small crosshair cursor appears on the screen. Click the first mouse button twice: once for the first corner of the rectangle, a second time for

---

TIP NUMBER 15
On Conversion Losses

As in DOS-based file translation, the conversion may not be 100% accurate. If you copy a paragraph from Windows Write that has normal, bold, and italic text, you paste the paragraph into another Windows application without loosing the bolding and italics—but only if the application understands Write's bold and italic codes.

   AutoCAD doesn't, so bringing the Write text into an AutoCAD drawing loses the text attributes. As the workaround, use AutoCAD's single format code %%u for underlining. ■

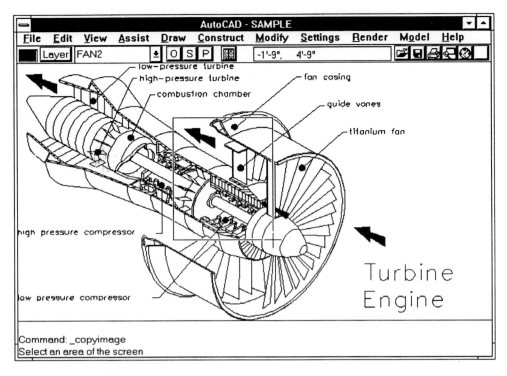

the other corner (see Figure). You can include the Toolbar, the side screen menu, and the Command: prompt area in the rectangle.

5. Start the Windows Write program. For this tutorial, load a text file, such as Maint.Wri found in the \Acadwin\Vb\Asvu subdirectory.

6. Position the I-beam cursor at the place in the document where you want the picture positioned. Pick **Edit** from the menu bar, then select the **Paste** command. The image is automatically copied from the Clipboard to the Write document (see Figure).

7. To edit the picture, click on it with the mouse's left button; the figure will turn to reverse video (white lines on black background). Once the figure is selected, you can then:

 ▸ Delete the figure by pressing the **<Del>** key.

 ▸ Move the figure by first pressing **<Shift><Del>**, repositioning the I-beam cursor, then pressing **<Shift><Ins>**.

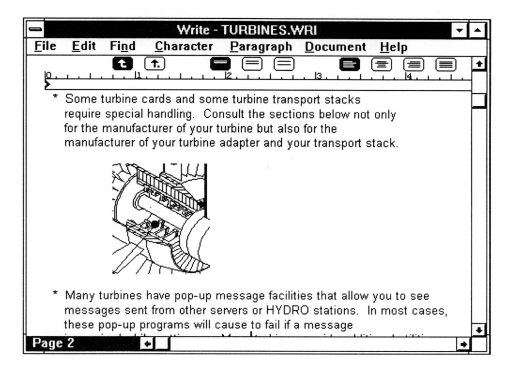

The figure shows a Windows Write application window titled "Write - TURBINES.WRI" with menu items File, Edit, Find, Character, Paragraph, Document, Help. The document text reads:

* Some turbine cards and some turbine transport stacks require special handling. Consult the sections below not only for the manufacturer of your turbine but also for the manufacturer of your turbine adapter and your transport stack.

* Many turbines have pop-up message facilities that allow you to see messages sent from other servers or HYDRO stations. In most cases, these pop-up programs will cause to fail if a message

Page 2

▸ Copy the figure by first pressing **<Ctrl><Ins>,** repositioning the I-beam cursor, then pressing **<Shift><Ins>.**

▸ Position the figure horizontally via the **Paragraph** menu; you can change the justification (left, center, or right) and change the indentation.

▸ Change the figure size in Write via the **Edit** menu; select the **Size Picture** item. The figure is outlined by a grey box and the cursor changes to a square. Grab one edge of the box and move it. The box changes size and the figure resizes itself.

Remember to save your work!

Tutorial 2
Copying Vectors from AutoCAD

Here is how to copy a vector image from AutoCAD to the Windows Clipboard:

1. The **Copy Vectors** command lets select AutoCAD entities. If you want to select everything in the drawing, use the All option. From the **Edit** menu, select the **Copy Vectors** item or use the CopyClip command, as follows:

   ```
   Command: copyclip
   Select objects: all
   Select objects: <Enter>
   ```

   Unlike the **Copy Image** command, you cannot include the Tool Bar, the side screen menu, or the Command: prompt area in the rectangle—just AutoCAD entities. If you want to copy a detail, the selection process is easier if you zoom in on the detail. Then use the Crossing, Window, or any other selection mode.

2. Switch to Windows Write and use the **Edit | Paste** command to place the vector graphic in the text. You can edit the drawing in Write using the steps listed in Tutorial 1.

TIP NUMBER 16
On Using Gray

If you want to specifically use shades of gray, you will need to learn how AutoCAD colors map to your printer's shades of gray. The şlide file, ColorWh.Sld, displays all of AutoCAD's 256 colors mapped to the ACI (AutoCAD color index) number. ■

Tutorial 3
Pasting Text into AutoCAD

AutoCAD for Windows lets you insert text into a drawing from the Windows Clipboard. The Figure below shows the three lines of text highlighted in black in the Windows Write word processor (bottom); the copied text in the Clipboard (right center); the text inserted into AutoCAD with the **DText** command, top.

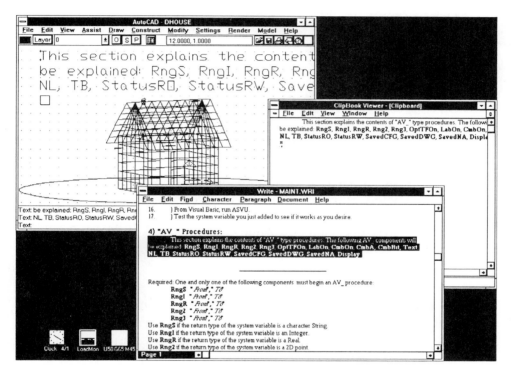

1. Start Windows Write and open a text file, such as Maint.Wri (used in Tutorial 1).

2. Select at least two lines of text.

3. Use the **Edit | Copy** command to copy the highlighted text to the Clipboard.

4. Switch to AutoCAD. Before you can use the **Paste Command** command to insert text into the drawing, you *must* first start AutoCAD's **DText** command and set the justification, style, insertion point, text height and

rotation angle, as follows:

```
Command: dtext
Justify/Style/<Start point>: <pick>
Height <0.2000>: <Enter>
Rotation <0.0000>: <Enter>
Text:
```

5. When you get the Text: prompt, pick **Edit** from the menu bar and then select the **Paste Command** command, as follows:

```
Text: <Edit> <Paste Command>
Text: <Enter>
Command:
```

The text flows onto the drawing using the current Style setting; format codes are not translated. The Figure shows that AutoCAD did not paste the tab and the bold portions of the text.

6. When the **Paste Text** command is finished, press <Enter> to end the **DText** command.

Tutorial 4
Pasting Vectors into AutoCAD

In this tutorial, we look at pasting a vector image from the Clipboard into an AutoCAD drawing. Of AutoCAD's four interactions with the Clipboard, pasting vectors is the most complex because of the many options available to the user.

The format that Windows uses to share vector-based drawings between applications is called WMF, short for Windows MetaFile. However, not all applications provide or accept files in WMF format; Windows does not come bundled with any vector-oriented drawing applications. For this tutorial, you need a third-party application that can copy vectors to the Clipboard. Among such applications are:

- ► **CAD Programs** such as AutoSketch for Windows, 3D Concepts for Windows, Cadvance for Windows, Drafix CAD Windows, GFA-CAD for Windows, TurboCAD Professional for Windows, and Ultimate CAD for Windows.

- ► **Near-CAD Programs** such as Mannequin Designer, Intellidraw, Visio, and Alias Upfront.

- ► **Drawing, Illustration and Charting Programs** such as Arts & Letters, CorelDraw, Illustrator, Micrografix, and Excel.

The Paintbrush application supplied with Windows is a raster-based drawing application. It's advantage is that it accepts WMF images from the Clipboard and instantly converts them into raster. Be aware, though, that it has bugs in its PCX import and export functions, ranging from color palette shifting to blackouts.

TIP NUMBER 18
Clipboard Aspect Ratio

If you look at the vector image in the Clipboard (or Clipbook) Viewer, it may appear to have the wrong aspect ratio—it looks elongated or squashed. Don't worry; that just Windows fitting the vector image to fit the Clipboard Viewer window. When you bring the image into the destination application, the aspect ration is correct. ■

For this tutorial, we use Arts & Letters, a bezier-curve-based drawing program. In the Figure below, you see the same drawing from Arts & Letters (bottom), in the Clipboard Viewer (right middle), and in AutoCAD.

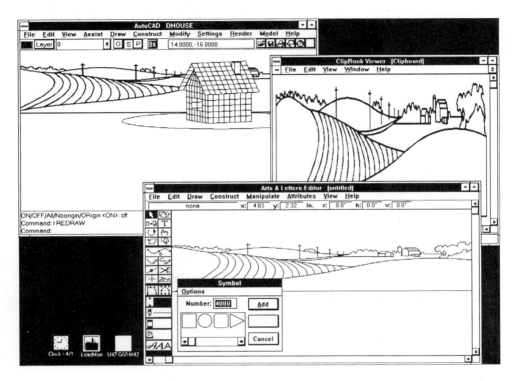

1. Start Arts & Letters (or other vector-based drawing package) and open a drawing. Arts & Letters come with a symbol library of several thousand ready-to-use drawings. Here I use symbol 4080, the countryside landscape.

2. Select the drawing with the selection tool.

3. Copy the drawing to the Clipboard with the **Edit | Copy** command.

4. Switch to AutoCAD. Before inserting the drawing, there are two options to set. Select the **File | Input/Output | WMF In Options...** command. The **WMF Options** dialogue box appears (see Figure, next page).

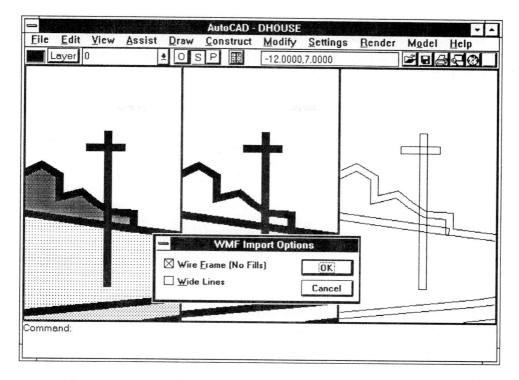

By clicking on the two check boxes, you let AutoCAD convert the WMF file in three different styles:

- **Wireframe off, wide lines on** (left panel, in Figure) imports the WMF drawing with areas and wide lines filled; this option takes the longest time to import.

- **Wireframe on, wide lines on** (center panel, in Figure) imports the WMF drawing with wide lines filled but no filled areas.

- **Wireframe on, wide lines off** (right panel, in Figure) imports the WMF drawing with wide lines outlined and no filled areas; this option takes the shortest time to import.

5. Import the WMF drawing with the **PasteClip** command or by selecting **Edit | Paste** from the menu, as follows:

```
Command: pasteclip
```

A small dialogue box appears on the screen (see Figure). The bar chart tracks AutoCAD's progress converting the WMF image to an AutoCAD-format block. Wait until AutoCAD is finished.

```
Loading Metafile...            Cancel
D:\ACADWIN\FARMLAND.WMF
[████████████████          ]
```

6. AutoCAD automatically launches the Insert command to insert the newly converted block, as follows:

```
Command: _INSERT Block name (or ?) <WMF0>: WMF1
Insertion point: 0,0
X scale factor <1> / Corner / XYZ: 1
Y scale factor (default=X): 1
Rotation angle <0>: 0
```

AutoCAD names the converted picture the name WMF*n*, where *n* starts at 0 (zero) and increments by one: WMF0, WMF1, etc.

7. AutoCAD places the WMF image in the drawing as a block. To edit the image, use the **Explode** command. AutoCAD explodes the block into polylines, which makes it convenient to edit the individual parts of the imported drawing,as follows:

```
Command: explode
Select objects: <pick WMFn block>
1 selected. Select objects: <Enter>
```

Tip Number 19
Flaky WMF Import

AutoCAD was not always predictable with the **PasteClip** command. For predictable results, answer the **Insert** command's prompts with actual values, rather than pressing **<Enter>** to agree with the default values provided by AutoCAD. Pressing just **<Enter>** makes AutoCAD insert the WMFn block at an unexpected insertion points, with strange scale factors, and at an odd rotation angle.

Instead of the lower left corner, the insertion point of the WMFn block is located at the upper left corner. Thus, if you insert the WMFn block at (0,0), it may not appear on the screen. Do a Zoom Extents after AutoCAD has finished placing the block. ■

---

8. In addition to using the Clipboard, you import WMF drawings with the **WMFin** command, as follows:

Command: **wmfin**

AutoCAD displays the **WMF In** dialogue box (see Figure). This dialogue box has a unique preview feature. Click once on the WMF filename to preview the image in full color.

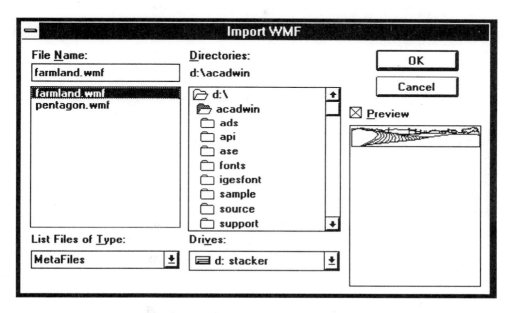

When you click the **OK** button, AutoCAD uses the same **Insert-** command sequence as with the **PasteClip** command.

TIP NUMBER 20
Where'd that Clip Go?

The Windows Clipboard can only handle one clip at a time. The next use of the **Cut** or **Copy** command a replaces the previous contents of the Clipboard. Either use the **Edit | Paste** command right away or use the Clipboard's **File | Save As** command to save the contents of the Clipboard to a CLP file on disk.

  If you use Windows for Workgroups, the ClipBook Viewer save multiple clips with its **Edit | Paste** command. ■

> Tip Number 21
> ## Clipboard Short-cut Keys
>
> If you do a lot of cutting and pasting, you might find it faster to use the keyboard. The keyboard equivalents to the **Cut**, **Copy**, and **Paste** commands vary depending on the application:
>
> ▸ For the **Cut** command, press **\<Shift>\<Del>**, or **\<Ctrl>-X**, or **\<Alt>-E-U**
>
> ▸ For the **Copy** command, press **\<Ctrl>\<Ins>**, or **\<Ctrl>-C**, or **\<Alt>-E-C**
>
> ▸ For the **Paste** command, press **\<Shift>\<Ins>**, or **\<Ctrl>-V**, or **\<Alt>-E-P**
>
> In general, older applications use the **\<Shift>\<Del>**, etc, keystrokes, while newer applications use **\<Ctrl>-X**. All use the **\<Alt>** key combination. ∎

Summary

In this chapter, you learned how to use the Windows Clipboard with AutoCAD. You copied and pasted raster images, vector pictures, and text. In the next chapter, you learn how to exercise your knowledge of the Clipboard to practical applications.

5

Integrating Applications

*I*ndividualism is out; integration is in. Because of Windows, applications no longer stand alone. Instead, they cooperate. No longer can data be proprietary; it is a commodity to be freely shared. The previous chapters described how to exchange images between AutoCAD and the Windows Clipboard. Later chapters describe how to share data. This chapter covers how to integrate AutoCAD graphics with other Windows applications.

Executive Summary

In this chapter, we look at how the Clipboard lets AutoCAD integrate with other Windows applications. Step-by-step tutorials show you how to use the following products:

Image-In-Color Professional
- High-end raster editor that works with color, gray shade and bilevel monochrome images
- Clipboard import from AutoCAD: BMP (bitmap) raster format
- Clipboard export to AutoCAD: none (raster format is not supported by AutoCAD)

Arts & Letters
- High-end, bezier-curve editor that works in color or gray shade
- Includes thousands of symbols and dozens of fonts
- Clipboard import from AutoCAD: BMP (bitmap) raster and WMF (metafile) vector format
- Clipboard export to AutoCAD: WMF format

AutoSketch for Windows
- Low-end CAD software for two-dimensional design
- Clipboard import from AutoCAD: none (Clipboard import supported only for AutoSketch-format objects)
- Clipboard export to AutoCAD: WMF (metafile) vector format

Starting in AutoCAD

To look at how other graphics applications interact with AutoCAD, load the Kitchen2 drawing, a 3D sample drawing found in the subdirectory \Acadwin\Tutorial. The drawing is of a kitchen and adjacent dining room.

1. There are four viewports; pick the perspective view of the kitchen and reduce the viewports to one, as follows:

   Command: **vports si**

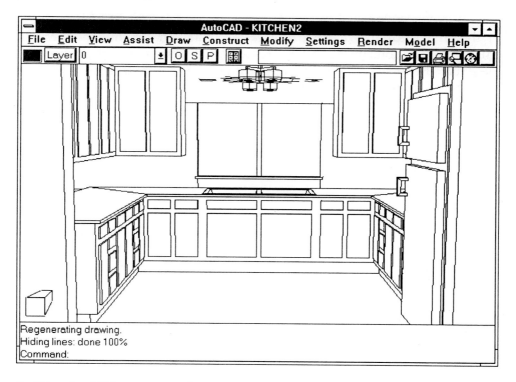

2. Use the Hide command to remove the hidden lines and eliminate the "see-through" wireframe look:

   Command: **hide**

3. Having decided on the view of the drawing, you have several options for exporting the view. AutoCAD gives you the option of exporting the image in two different formats. Both are listed in the **Edit** menu:

   ▸ To copy the image in raster format, use the **Copy Image** command

   ▸ To retain the image in vector format, use the **Copy Vectors** command

   Once in the Clipboard, you paste the image into other Windows applications.

In the first tutorial, we paste the raster image in the Image-In raster editing application. In the second tutorial, we paste the vector image in the Arts & Letters vector editing application. In the final tutorial, we paste an AutoSketch vector image into AutoCAD.

TIP NUMBER 22
Working with Monochrome Images

Most desktop publishing work is done in black-and-white, also known as "monochrome." AutoCAD has a useful feature for converting all drawing vectors from color into black.

Select the **File | Preferences...** command to display the **Preference's** dialogue box. Click on the **Colors...** button, the click on the **Monochrome vectors** check box.

Your drawing changes from color to black-and-white, which makes it much easier to import the image into monochrome documents. ■

Tutorial 1
Working with AutoCAD Raster Images

Image-In-Color is a powerful raster editor and is developed by CPI of Switzerland. Image-In-Color Professional can handle 24-bit color, 256-scale gray shade, and line art. It has dozens of tools and special effects, such as motion blur, embossing, sharpen, black hole, and ripple. Image-In handles TIFF, PCX, TGA, GIF, MSP, IMG, and BMP as input and output formats. Image-In supports MDI (the Windows multiple document interface) so that you can load multiple images at a time.

Image-In ColorPro

1. In AutoCAD, copy the kitchen image to the Windows Clipboard in raster format with **Edit | Copy Image**. Select the entire kitchen area.

2. Start Image-In-Color and bring in the kitchen image from the Clipboard with **Edit | Paste to New**. This places the contents of the Clipboard into a new image frame (see Figure).

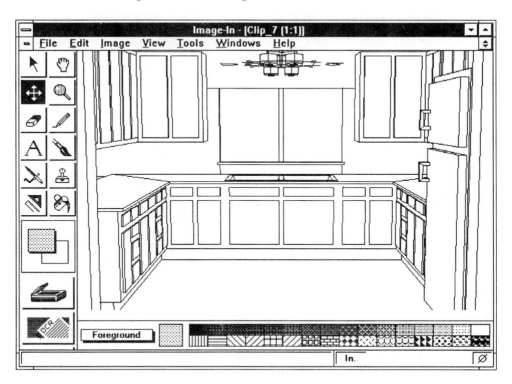

3. Once placed in Image-In, or other raster editor, you must decide on the image's ultimate destination. That determines the tools you work with. With Image-In-Color, you have three choices—color, gray shade and monochrome—found in the **Image | Convert to >** menu:

   ▶ **Do nothing** to keep the image in its original colors. For magazine work, I leave the screen grabs in their original colors.

   ▶ **Image | Convert to > | Gray Scale...** converts the color image to 256 shades of grey.

   ▶ **Image | Convert to > | Bilevel...** converts the color image to black-and-white. For book work, such as this book, I convert screen grabs to bilevel monochrome.

4. When you convert the image to bilevel monochrome, Image-In-Color has three choices in conversion done—threshold, halftone, and error diffusion (see Figure):

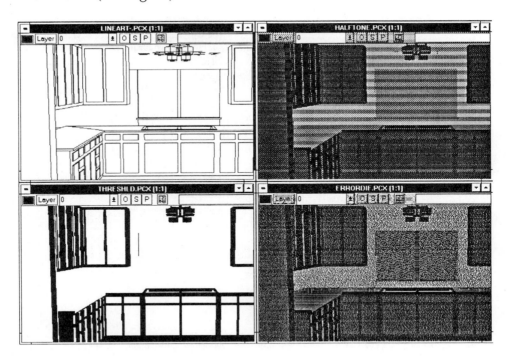

- **Threshold** converts all colors to black or white. This is best for line art and creates the clearest image for technical documentation (upper left in Figure). At the default threshold level of 50, all darker colors are converted to black, while all lighter colors are converted to white. (Threshold=50 is the value I use in converting most screen grabs to figures for this book.) A lower threshold level, such as 10, converts more dark colors to white' a higher level, such as 90, converts more lighter colors to black.

- **Halftone** converts colors into many tiny dots. The effect is similar to black-and-white photographs in newspapers. By making the dots different sizes, halftone simulates the effect of gray shading (upper right in Figure). Image-In-Color lets you use dots, lines, ellipsis, or diamond shapes at any angle and frequency.

- **Error diffusion** converts all colors into many tiny dots. The difference from halftone is that the dots are all the same size but differ in density. The effect is used by Apple's monochrome Powerbook computers to simulate shades of gray (lower left in Figure).

4. As an alternative to Image-In-Color's automatic monochrome conversion, you can do it yourself.

   To create the shaded drawing shown above, I touched up the

kitchen image by using the pen tool to close up some gaps in the line work. I used the flood-area tool to fill areas of the kitchen with shades of gray, selected from the palette at the bottom of the screen. If I need to reuse a shade, the dropper tool picks up an existing shade and assigns it to the flood-area tool. For detail work of small areas, the magnifying glass enlarges the image in powers of two, up to 16x.

These techniques took only a few minutes to enhance the AutoCAD kitchen image. Once done, I saved the shaded image as a PCX file, then imported it into WordPerfect.

Image-In-Color Professional
Image-In, Inc.
406 East 79th Street
Minneapolis, MN 55420

Tip Number 23
Windows Screen Capture

Image-In helped me create the screen images used in this book. I press the <Print Screen> key, which under Windows captures the entire screen to the Clipboard. If you want to capture the uppermost window, press **<Alt>-<Print** Screen>.

After capturing the screen, I switch to Image-In with the **<Alt>-<Tab>** key. Then I follow the process described above. When gray shades are important, I use the **Image | Convert to > | Grayscale** command and experiment with converting to half-toning or error diffusion, with plenty of applications of the **Edit | Undo** command.

If I need just a portion of the screen grab, I use the selection tool to window the area of interest, then use the **Edit | Cut** command, following with an **Edit | Paste to New**. Sometimes screen grabs needed touching up; I use the magnifying glass and the pen tool to fix things up.

Finally, I save the images as PCX files on disk using the **File | Save As...** command. ▪

Tutorial 2
Editing AutoCAD Vector Drawings

Graphics Editor Arts & Letters is one of several Bezier-curve-based drawing packages available for Windows. Arts & Letters is known for its collection of 3,500 predrawn pieces of clip-art. This drawing package is stands halfway between raster-based drawing software (such as Image-In-Color) and vector-based software, such as AutoCAD. All images are drawn with Bezier curves. You manipulate objects using control points, like a CAD package. You floodfill areas with color and patterns, like a raster software.

1. In AutoCAD, copy the kitchen image to the Clipboard in vector format with the **Edit | Copy Vectors** command. Select the entire kitchen area.

2. Start Arts & Letters and bring the kitchen image in from the Clipboard with the **Edit | Paste** command. This places the contents of the Clipboard into the Arts & Letters editing screen (see Figure).

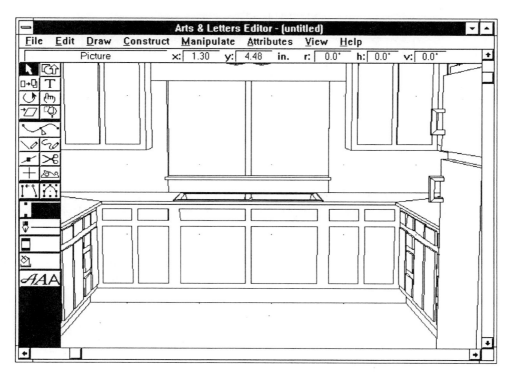

3. Unfortunately, the AutoCAD image (which is in Windows Metafile format) can only be resized; Arts & Letters cannot edit it, such as changing the color or converting it to *freeform* (Arts & Letters' individual vectors). I selected images from the clip-art collection and placed them on top of the kitchen: the man at the table, the flowers in the window, the hanging plants, the food processor, and watermelon on the kitchen counter (see Figure below). These techniques took only a few minutes to embellish the AutoCAD-drawn kitchen. Here are some tips:

- ▶ Use the **Draw | Symbol...** command to specify a symbol's number; refer to the Arts & Letters *Clip Art Handbook* for symbol reference numbers.

- ▶ To maintain the "hidden-line removal" look, use the **Attributes | Fill...** command's Solid option, along with the **Attributes | Color...** command's White option.

- ▶ To move symbols in front of or behind each other, select the symbol, then use the **Manipulate | Stacking Order >** command.

▶ To create a bit of variety when working with copies of symbols, such as the hanging plants, use the **Manipulate | Flip | Horizontally** command to make a mirror image.

▶ Once done, I export the image as a TIFF file with the **File | Export...** command; the EPS format takes up ten times as much disk space, while the CGM and WPG formats don't correctly export the AutoCAD portion of the image.

Arts & Letters
Computer Support Corp.
15926 Midway Road
Dallas, TX 75244

Tutorial 3
Importing Blocks into AutoCAD

[fig: need bmp logo here] AutoSketch for Windows is Autodesk's low-end CAD software for two-dimensional design. AutoSketch has significant limitations for drafters: ten layers, weak macro programming language, and few third-party products. However, AutoSketch paved the way for the improvements seen in Release 12 for Windows. Features like the Aerial View, Toolbox, two-way Clipboard support, and OLE server were implemented in AutoSketch a year prior to AutoCAD (see Figure).

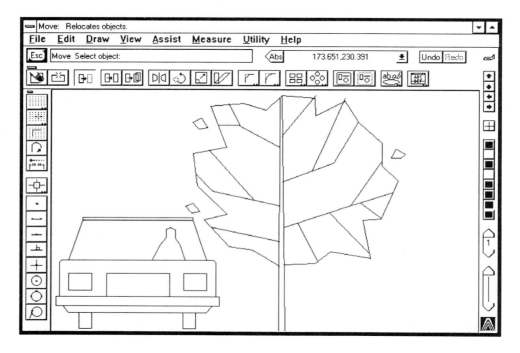

AutoSketch for Windows comes with 2,000 blocks (called "parts" by AutoSketch). We take advantage of the large symbol library and the Windows Clipboard to import them into AutoCAD.

AutoSketch sends BMP raster and WMF vector drawings to the Clipboard; it does not paste either format from the Clipboard. You can use the Clipboard to copy and paste AutoSketch objects into SKD drawings. In this tutorial, we copy an AutoSketch block to AutoCAD in WMF format, thus bypassing the double-translation required by DXF.

1. Start AutoSketch for Windows.

2. Look the library of parts (the AutoSketch name for "blocks") with the **Draw | Part...** command. AutoSketch displays the **Select Part File** dialogue box (see Figure)

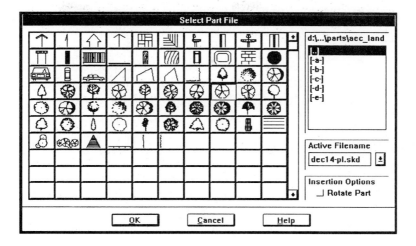

3. Select a block by double-clicking on its picture. (If only AutoCAD had this graphical of block library interface!)

4. AutoSketch prompts you to select an insertion point, as follows:

        Part To point: **<pick>**

5. If you want, change the block's characteristics, such as its color or aspect ratio or edit details of the block.

6. Copy the block to the Clipboard with the **Utility | Copy Metafile**, as follows:

        Copy Metafile Select object: **<pick>**

    (Curiously, AutoSketch has its Clipboard copy and paste commands in the Utility menu rather than the standard Edit menu.)

7. Switch to AutoCAD and insert the block with the **Edit | Paste** command.

The imported block has retained its vector advantages. You can edit the block as you would any other entity. Using the Clipboard to transfer blocks from AutoSketch (and other CAD packages) to AutoCAD is faster than DXF.

AutoSketch's other Clipboard-related commands are:

▸ **Utility | Copy Bitmap** copies objects to the Clipboard in BMP raster format.

▸ **Utility | Copy Objects** copies objects to the Clipboard in WMF, native and ownerlink vector formats. *Native* format means the objects are stored in AutoSketch's SKD format; *ownerlink* format means the objects can be linked to a Windows OLE client application.

▸ **Utility | Paste Objects** pastes native-format objects from the Clipboard to the AutoSketch drawing.

AutoSketch for Windows
Autodesk Retail Products
11911 North Creek Parkway South
Bothell, WA 98011

Summary

In this chapter, you learned how to apply the Windows Clipboard to three Windows applications and AutoCAD. In the next chapter, you learn about object linking and embedding, an semi-automatic form of copy-and-paste.

Object Linking and Embedding

*E*nter OLE: object linking and embedding. Instead of placing an AutoCAD drawing in another application with the Clipboard, OLE lets you set up a link that lets you easily edit the figure. In this chapter, we explain OLE and how it works. We work through step-by-step examples by linking an AutoCAD drawing with two common OLE-aware applications. We also look at object packaging, a simpler form of OLE.

Executive Summary

Windows OLE (object linking and embedding) is easy to use—except when it comes to remembering the sequence of menu selections. Here is a summary of the steps involved in setting up an OLE link between two Windows applications:

- **To embed an AutoCAD drawing in another Windows applications:**

  1. **Select Objects:** In the OLE server (such as AutoCAD Release 12 for Windows), select the drawing entities with the **Edit | Copy Embed** command.

  2. **To Embed:** In the OLE client (such as Windows Write), embed the drawing with the **Edit | Paste** command.

  3. **To Edit:** In Write, double-click on the drawing to return to the OLE server. When finished editing, update the drawing with AutoCAD's **File | Update** command.

- **To link an AutoCAD drawing in another Windows applications:**

  1. **Select Objects:** In the OLE server (such as AutoCAD), select the drawing entities with the **Edit | Copy Link** command.

  2. **To Link:** Link the AutoCAD drawing in the OLE client document with the **Edit | Paste Link** command.

  3. **To Edit:** In Write, double-click on the drawing to return to the OLE server. When finished editing, update the drawing with Cardfile's **File | Restore** command.

- **To change the OLE link:** In the OLE client (Write), change the nature of the link with the **Edit | Links...** dialogue box.

What is OLE?

When you use the charting feature in Excel or another Windows spreadsheet, you use OLE (object linking and embedding)—perhaps unknowingly. When you double-click on the chart, Excel switches to its charting module. When you change a value in the spreadsheet, the chart automatically updates itself.

That's all done via OLE, while the underlying mechanism is actually DDE (dynamic data exchange; see the "Dynamic Data Exchange" chapter) with the dirty details hidden from the user.

OLE performs two functions: (1) it links and (2) it embeds. Think of linking and embedding objects as an intelligent application of the hand-operated Clipboard copy-and-paste process. First, let's define the terms *object*, *link*, and *embed*.

OLE Objects. An *object* is a piece of text, a range of spreadsheet cells, a picture, a video clip, or a sound bite. Sometimes you see the actual object, such as spreadsheet cells (see Figure). Other times, an icon represents the object, such as a sound bite shown as the microphone icon.

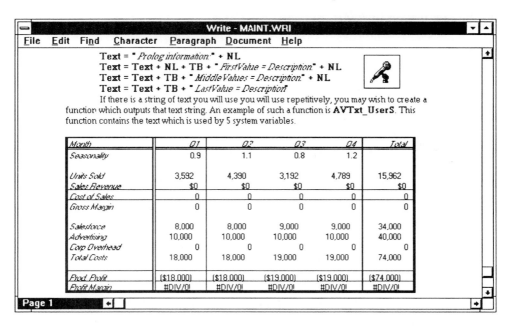

Not everything in Windows is an OLE object. The Windows application program must be *OLE-aware*, which means its programmers added OLE capabilities. OLE-aware programs include CorelDraw, AutoSketch for Windows, Cadvance for Windows, Visio, WordPerfect, and Excel.

AutoCAD Release 12 for Windows' OLE object is a *picture*. Picture is the Windows name for a vector drawing. AutoCAD converts the drawing into picture objects of five formats:

▸ Raster image in BMP (bitmap) format

▸ Vector image in WMF (Windows metafile) format

▸ Vector image in DWG (AutoCAD drawing) format

▸ Linked vector image in ObjectLink format

▸ Object originator information in OwnerLink format

Not all OLE-aware programs are equal. There are, in fact, four kinds of OLE-aware applications:

1. **OLE server** programs provide objects but do not accept objects. Windows Paintbrush, the Sound Recorder, AutoCAD, and AutoSketch are OLE servers.

2. **OLE client** programs accept objects but do not provide them. Windows Write, Cardfile, and WordPerfect are OLE clients.

3. **OLE server and client** programs provide objects and accept objects. Microsoft Excel, CorelDraw, and Cadvance for Windows are OLE clients and servers.

4. **OLE-only** programs operate only under OLE; you cannot launch them on their own. WordArt is a Windows application that runs as an OLE server from within an OLE client.

Object Linking. When an object is *linked* from one OLE application to another, Windows maintains a live line of communications between the two applications. When you change the object in the OLE server application, the linked object automatically updates in the OLE client application. Clearly, this real-time updating lends itself to powerful relationships in compound documents, as shown by Microsoft Excel charts.

Object Embedding. You may not want an object updating itself via OLE linking. For this reason, Windows provides a second form of OLE called embedding. When an object is *embedded* into another application, there is no automatic updating. Instead, you manually update the object.

The difference between linking and embedding is that linking allows automatic updates, while embedding requires you to manually initiate the update. You can switch between automatic and manual updating.

The Windows OLE system uses Clipboard and DDE to perform its work. It is helpful to keep the Clipboard Viewer (or the ClipBook Viewer, if you are using the Windows for Workgroups) open as you work through the tutorial. The open Clipboard performs two functions: (1) you instantly confirm that the copy function worked and (2) you inspect the formats of the copied object.

OLE in AutoCAD for Windows

As we saw in the "Windows Clipboard" chapter, AutoCAD Release 12 for Windows has six commands in the **Edit** menu that work with the Clipboard. Two commands are expressly for OLE commands; a third OLE-related command shows up in the **File** menu:

1. **Copy Link** is similar to **Edit | Copy Vectors** but is used for OLE purposes. Selected entities are copied in five formats: WMF (called "picture" in the Clipboard Viewer), DWG ("native"), bitmap, palette, and OwnerLink. In macros, you use the new **CopyLink** command.

2. **Copy Embed** is similar to **Copy Link** but initiates OLE's embedding procedure. The entire drawing is copied in four formats: picture, native, OwnerLink, and ObjectLink. Macros use the **CopyEmbed** command.

3. **Update** only appears the **File** menu after AutoCAD has been launched

by an OLE client application. Use this command to update the AutoCAD drawing in the client. There is no command for use in macros.

Once copied to the Clipboard, the picture is placed in any OLE-client application. You recognize an OLE client by its **Edit** menu: there are two or more versions of the Paste command. **Paste**, **Paste Link** and **Paste Special...** are common examples (see Figure).

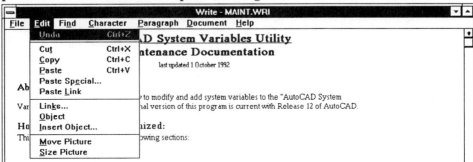

Here's the difference between the three Paste commands:

1. **Paste** uses OLE to *embed* the picture if it came from an OLE server, such as AutoCAD. If the picture came from an application that was not an OLE server, then it is pasted in the usual static cut'n paste manner.

2. **Paste Link** *links* the picture between the OLE server (such as AutoCAD) and the OLE client, such as Write.

3. **Paste Special...** isn't special at all. Instead, it displays a dialogue box that gives you a choice between using the **Paste** and **Paste Link** commands (seee Figure). It lists the choice of object formats available.

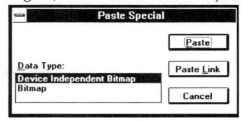

Think of **Paste Special** as the dialogue box version of the **Paste** and **Paste Link** command combined together. With this background in OLE, let's practice embedding an AutoCAD drawing into Windows Write.

Tutorial 1
Embed AutoCAD Drawings in Windows Write

In the first tutorial, we use OLE to embed an AutoCAD drawing into a Write document.

1. Start AutoCAD for Windows and open a drawing, such as Dim.Dwg located in the \AcadWin\Tutorial subdirectory.

2. Copy the drawing to the Clipboard with the **Edit | Copy Embed** command. AutoCAD prompts you twice, as follows:

   ```
   Select objects: all
   Select objects: <Enter>
   ```

   Use the All option to select the entire drawing; AutoCAD highlights the selected objects. When you press **<Enter>**, AutoCAD unhighlights the objects and places the picture in the Clipboard (see Figure).

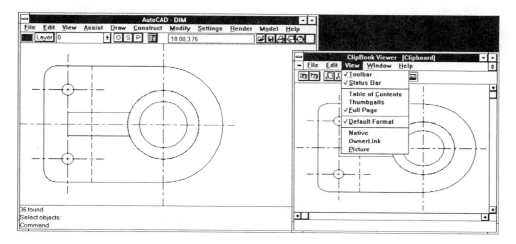

3. Start Write and load in a document with a WRI extension, such as Maint.Wri supplied with AutoCAD for Windows in the subdirectory \Acadwin\Vb\Asvu.

4. In Write, select **Edit | Paste**. Windows places the Dim.Dwg into the Write document (see Figure).

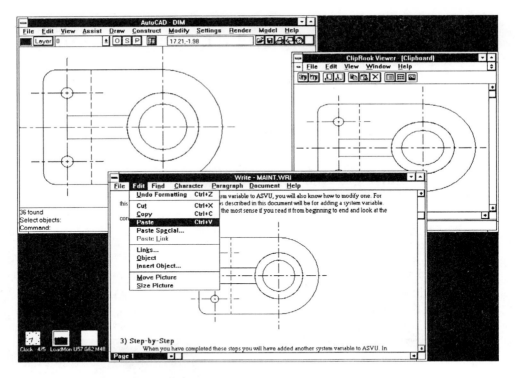

Notice that in Write's **Edit** menu the **Paste Link** item is grayed out; Windows is telling you that OLE is being set up as embedding and *not* as linking.

5. The AutoCAD picture is now placed in the Write document. We edit it with Write and with AutoCAD. Write has two commands that move and size the picture; AutoCAD is needed to edit everything else in the picture.

Select the picture by clicking once on it with the mouse's left button. Write highlights the selected picture by making the background black (see Figure).

TIP NUMBER 24
Frozen Layers Not Linked

AutoCAD does not copy the contents of frozen layers to the Clipboard. Thus, when you come back to AutoCAD after linking or embedding a drawing, you cannot thaw frozen layers since they do not exist. ∎

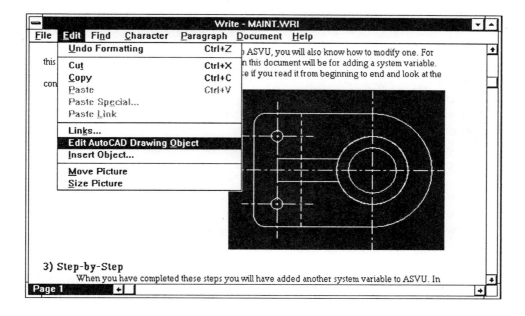

6. In the **Edit** menu, select the **Move Picture** or **Size Picture** command. When you do, Write unhighlights the picture and surrounds the graphic with a gray box. At the same time, the arrow cursor changes to the boxy Move-Size cursor.

7. As you move the mouse, the picture moves or resizes. When you click the mouse button, the picture is put in place.

8. To edit the drawing back in AutoCAD, double-click on the picture. When you do, Windows instructs AutoCAD to load the embedded drawing. AutoCAD uses the undocumented **FileOpen** command, which opens a drawing file without using a dialogue box. As the drawing loads, keep an eye on the Command: prompt area:

Tip Number 25
Fast Picture Justification

As an alternative to the move and size commands, you can use the **Paragraph | Left, Centered** and **Right** commands to position the picture in the center or up against the left and right margins. These commands work only if the picture is smaller than the width between margins. ∎

```
Command: fileopen
Enter name of drawing <C:\ACADWIN\TUTORIAL\DIM>:
  C:\acad062c.dwg
```

The drawing may look the same as the Dim.Dwg you began with the tutorial but now has a name such as Acad062c.Dwg or similar. When you use File Manager to look at the root directory, you see the Acad062c.Dwg file.

Here's why AutoCAD loads a copy rather than the original: back when you used the **Copy Embed** command, you might have selected only a portion of the drawing. AutoCAD could not reload the original drawing since the embedded drawing would be different. Still, all the elements of the original drawing are there: the colors, layers, and linetypes are all intact. That's another OLE advantage over using the Clipboard and WMF or BMP files.

As a reminder, the title bar shows that you are working with an OLE drawing; it reads: "AutoCAD - Drawing in Client Document."

9. Make a change to the drawing, such as changing colors and linetypes or dimensioning the drawing.

10. To update the changed drawing back in Write, select AutoCAD's **File | Update Client Document** command. (The **Update Client Document** command only appears in AutoCAD's **File** menu when you edit an OLE drawing.) AutoCAD uses the QSave command and the edited drawing replaces the original in Write (see Figure).

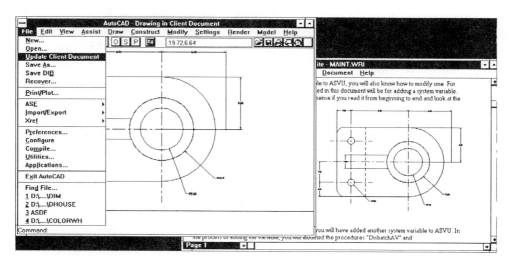

11. When you close the Write document, Write warns: "This document contains open embedded objects that may need updating. Do you want to update open embedded objects before closing?" (See Figure.)

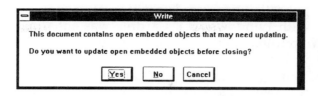

When you answer Yes, OLE causes AutoCAD to resend the drawing to Write.

A Different Way to Launch AutoCAD. In the tutorial, we first started AcadWin, then we started Write. As an alternative, we can use OLE to automatically launch AutoCAD from within Write—powerful stuff! Here's how:

1. Start Write and load a WRI document.

2. Select the **Edit | Insert Object...** command. Write displays the **Insert Object** dialogue box (see Figure).

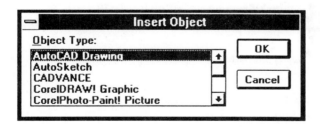

3. The **Object Type** list box shows that you can launch AutoCAD, AutoSketch, Cadvance, and CorelDraw to embed a figure—assuming those applications are loaded on your computer. Select "AutoCAD Drawing" and click the **OK** button.

4. Via OLE, Windows launches AutoCAD and waits for you to load a drawing. Open the Dim.Dwg and use **Edit | Copy Embed** command. From here on, the method is the same as in tutorial above: switch back to Write and use **Paste** to insert the picture.

Tutorial 2
Link AutoCAD Drawings to Windows Cardfile

The Cardfile application program lets you create a simple database of text and pictures. With Windows v3.1, Cardfile was enhanced to become an OLE client. We put that ability to good use by creating a drawing library of AutoCAD drawings.

Cardfile becomes an alternative to starting AutoCAD and selecting a drawing by subdirectory and filename. You visually select a drawing from the Cardfile, which automatically launches AutoCAD and the drawing.

Or, if you rather, Cardfile displays a list of drawing names (up to 39 characters long) in alphabetical order—a vast improvement over the DOS limit of eight characters!

The most exciting aspect to the Cardfile-OLE-AutoCAD link is that the contents of the Cardfile database are updated as AutoCAD drawings are changed. Once a drawing is added to the Cardfile database, you never need to update it.

In this tutorial, we link AutoCAD drawings to Cardfile.

1. Start Cardfile and create new cardfile with **File | New** (see Figure).

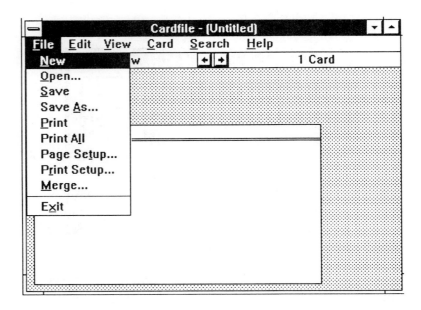

2. Switch Cardfile to picture mode by with **Edit | Picture**.

3. Launch AutoCAD via OLE with by clicking on **Edit | Insert Object...**, then select "AutoCAD Drawing" from the dialogue box.

4. After AutoCAD has finished loading, open a drawing such as Dim.Dwg, which we used in the previous tutorial.

5. Use AutoCAD's **Edit | Copy Link** command. The **CopyLink** command copies the whole drawing to the Clipboard.

6. Switch back to Cardfile and paste the drawing with **Edit | Paste Link** (see Figure).

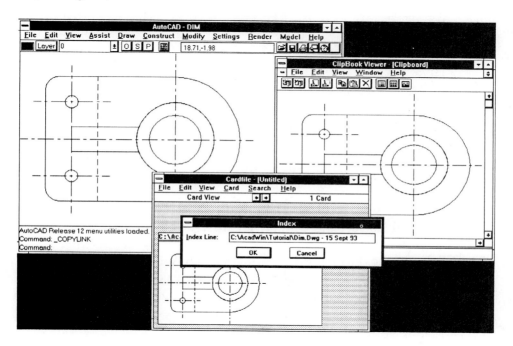

7. Give the card a name with the **Edit | Index...** command. The **Index** dialogue box appears. In the figure (above), I entered the drawing's location (C:\AcadWin\Tutorial\Dim.Dwg) and the date the card was created, 15 Sept 93.

8. If the 39-character limit to the index card is not enough, you add more text to the card by selecting **Edit | Text**. Cardfile switches back to text mode and lets you write text below the index line. The text overwrites the picture (see Figure).

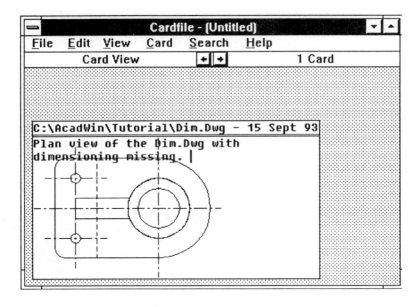

8. Save the CRD cardfile file with **File | Save As**, naming the file "Drawings.Crd."

9. Now we use Cardfile to launch AutoCAD with the selected drawing. Exit AutoCAD.

10. In Cardfile, select the Dim.Dwg card.

11. Click on the **Edit | Edit AutoCAD Drawing Object** command. Notice how Cardfile "knows" the picture was created by AutoCAD. OLE launches AutoCAD and opens the Dim.Dwg file. As soon AutoCAD finished loading the Dim.Dwg file, it uses OLE to update the copy of the drawing displayed by Cardfile.

12. Edit the drawing in AutoCAD, such as adding dimensions or stretching the widget.

13. To update the changes in the drawing, switch back to Cardfile. Select the **Edit | Restore** command. Just as the **Update** command only appears in AutoCAD when you edit an embedded drawing, the **Restore** command only appears in Cardfile when you edit a linked drawing. (If you make changes to the drawing but don't use the **Restore** command, the card is automatically updated next time you load AutoCAD.)

14. When you exit AutoCAD or close the drawing, OLE sometimes updates the link and sometimes it doesn't. Here's a summary:

   ▸ **No update** occurs with these AutoCAD commands: **End,** and **Quit** (without saving the changes),

   ▸ **Automatic update** occurs with these AutoCAD commands: **Quit** (with saving changes), **Save, SaveAs, New**

   If you open the Dim.Dwg in AutoCAD independent of Cardfile, none of AutoCAD's commands automatically update Cardfile. In this case, you have to use Cardfile's **Edit | Restore** command.

15. To add more cards to Cardfile, use the **Card | Add...** command. Remember to save your work!

Changing Links between Documents

Related to the **Paste Link** command is **Edit | Link**. The command displays the **Link** dialogue box that lets you adjust the link between AutoCAD, Write and other OLE-aware apps (see figure). The dialogue box lists the current links. It lets you update and cancel links, change the link information and switch link updating between automatic and manual.

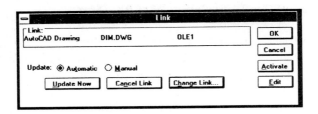

A Different Way to Edit the Picture

In the tutorials, you double-click on the picture to load it into AutoCAD. There is an alternative method:

1. Select the picture so that it turns black.

2. In the **Edit** menu, a new item shows up: **Edit AutoCAD Drawing Object**. Select it.

3. AutoCAD loads the Acad062c.Dwg (or a file with a similar name). From here on, the method is the same as in the tutorial above: make changes to the drawing and use AutoCAD's **File | Update Client Document** command.

Packaging Drawings as Icon Objects

Windows has an alternative to embedding drawings in documents called "Object Packager." Instead of embedding the actual AutoCAD drawing in the Write document, Object Packager lets you embed an icon representing the drawing in the document.

The advantage to the icon (called a "package" by Windows) is that the document works faster—scrolling through the document doesn't slow to a slothlike speed when it reaches the picture of the AutoCAD drawing. Some objects, such as sound clips and animations, are represented only as an icon in the document.

A drawback to the icon is that you no longer see the original drawing. A second drawback is that only OLE servers can be packaged in OLE clients. You can package an AutoCAD drawing as an icon in a Write document; you cannot package an icon in an AutoCAD drawing.

You insert the drawing as an icon into a document by two methods: (1) the fast way and (2) the controlled way. The fast way uses the mouse to drag the AutoCAD drawing file into the Write document. The controlled way uses the Object Packager application to control the appearance of the icon. The following tutorials describe both methods.

Tip Number 26
Hundreds of Icons

If you don't see an icon you like of those provided by the Program Manager, there are hundreds of other icons available in Windows. To access these icons, click on the **Insert Icon** dialogue box's **Browse...** button to open the **Browse** dialogue box. Load the file MorIcons.Dll. It contains slightly more than 100 icons, many of which are suitable for brand-name applications.

Other icons are hidden in Acad.Exe, DsDlWin.Dll, AcadApp.Exe, AcadDl.Exe, AcadPs.Exe, Ame.Exe, AToolBox.Exe, and AveRendr.Exe. The Figure shows the five icons available in Acad.Exe. ■

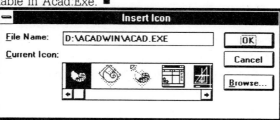

Tutorial 3
Packaging a Drawing, the Fast Method

The fast method of packaging an entire drawing uses the mouse to drag the DWG file into the Write document, as follows (see Figure):

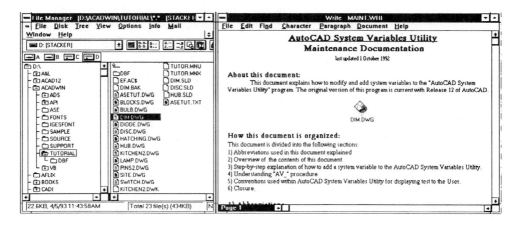

1. Start Write and open a document, such as Maint.Wri used in earlier tutorials.

2. Click the cursor at the point you want the package (icon) inserted.

3. Start File Manager and open the subdirectory where the prospective package resides, the drawing file in this case. For this tutorial, go to the \Acadwin\Tutorial subdirectory.

4. With the mouse, move the cursor over the Dim.Dwg filename.

5. Hold down the mouse button and drag the file icon to Write.

6. Release the mouse button. Windows inserts the default AutoCAD icon and prints the drawing's filename underneath.

In just a few seconds, you embedded an AutoCAD drawing into a Write document. So what do you do with it? If your office is networked, you can send the WRI file over electronic mail to an associate. They read the document and—if AutoCAD is available on the network—view the drawing by double-clicking on the icon.

Tutorial 4
Packaging a Drawing, the Controlled Method

The controlled method of packaging an object uses the Object Packager application (Packager.Exe). The Object Packager was added to Windows v3.1. It lets you control the look and wording of the icon (see Figure). Whereas the fast-method packages the entire file, the Object Packager lets you package part of a drawing.

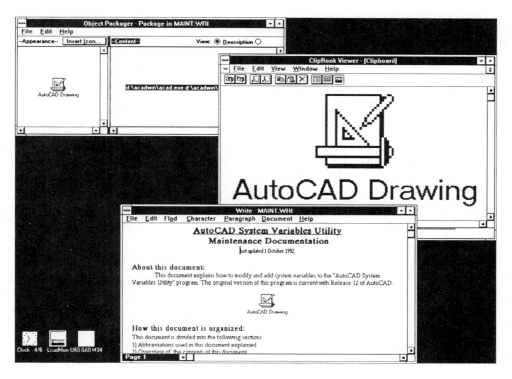

1. Start Write and open a document, such as Maint.Wri used in earlier tutorials.

2. Click the cursor at the point you want the package icon inserted.

3. Start Object Packager.

4. Click on the **Insert Icon...** button to open the **Insert Icon** dialogue box. Scroll through the selection of icons and click on the icon you want to use, then click on the **OK** button.

5. Now that you've chosen an icon, you specify the icon's label. Select the **Edit | Label...** command to display the **Label** dialogue box. Type a description of the icon, such as "AutoCAD Drawing." You are limited to 39 characters. Click **OK** when done.

6. With the icon's appearance set, you now specify the filename. Select the **Edit | Command Line...** command to display the **Command Line** dialogue box. Type in the filename with drive name and subdirectory path, such as "C:\Acadwin\Tutorial\Dim.Dwg." Click on **OK** when done. By specifying the filename, you package the entire drawing.

Or

If, instead, you want to package a portion of the Dim.Dwg, start AutoCAD and open the Dim.Dwg. Use the **Edit | Copy Embed** command and select a portion of the drawing. Switch to Object Packager and click on the **--Content--** window. Select the **Edit | Paste** command to insert the Dim.Dwg. To see the portion of the drawing, click on the **View | Picture** radio button (see Figure).

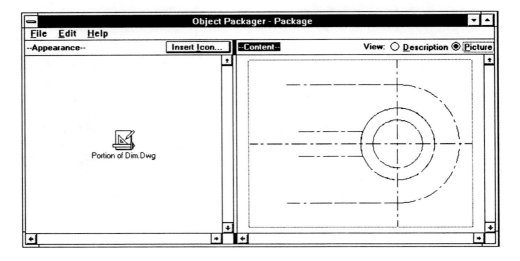

7. With the appearance and contents of the package set, select the **Edit | Copy Package** command to copy the package to the Clipboard.

8. Switch to Write and use the **Edit | Paste** command to insert the package's icon in the document at the current cursor location.

Tutorial 5
Using a Packaged Object

With the Dim.Dwg packaged as an icon in the Write document, you access the drawing within the object and edit the icon object, as follows:

1. To access the drawing within the object, double-click on its icon to launch AutoCAD with the Dim.Dwg. If you embedded part of the Dim.Dwg, then AutoCAD displays just the portion.

2. Make changes to the drawing, then use the **File** I **Update Client Document** command to return to the Write document.

3. To edit the icon object, click on the package's icon. It turns black.

4. Select the **Edit** I **Package Object >** I **Edit Package** command (see Figure). The command launches the Object Packager application and appears in the **Edit** menu only when you select a packaged object. Make changes to the package appearance and command line.

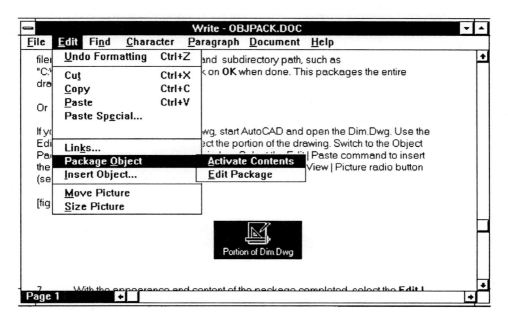

5. When finished, select the Object Packager's **File** I **Update** command.

OLE Pros and Cons

While OLE is a slick way to work with data, it has drawbacks. You cannot intuitively tell if a figure in a document was cut 'n paste in place or if is an OLE object. If it is an OLE object, you do not get back to the source if the link is broken. The OLE link is broken as easily as moving the source file to another subdirectory. OLE makes no attempt to locate a file with a broken link.

Windows uses many system resources to maintain the OLE links. According to the LoadMon utility, about 50% of the CPU load is used to maintain the real-time OLE links. Embedded drawings take up a lot of disk space. The few tutorial drawings (less than 100KB in DWG format) embedded into Cardfile create a CRD file of 1.3 MB—terribly inefficient.

Finally, there is the aesthetic problem. You may have noticed that Cardfile distorts vector pictures to a specific area, creating some odd aspect ratios. Some of these problems are be cured with OLE v2, which takes less memory and hogs fewer CPU resources.

Instead of working through a confusing set of menu selections (**Paste** versus **Paste Link** versus **Paste Special**, *et al.*), OLE v2 lets you drag and drop objects from one application to another.

When it comes time to edit, OLE v2-aware applications display a subset of the server's menu structure, rather than launch the entire program. In our example, that means Write would display AutoCAD's editing commands in Write's menu bar.

Windows has made us aware of how being able to share data among applications is more important than the applications themselves. OLE extends the concept to automate changes in the data and allows us to use one application within another, in effect making Windows applications add-ons to each other.

Summary

In this chapter, you learned about object linking and embedding. The tutorial showed you how to use OLE and the Object Packager. The next chapter describes commercial add-on software specific to AutoCAD for Windows.

Helpful Software

M any third-party add-ons written for the DOS version of AutoCAD work with AutoCAD for Windows. That's because they are written in AutoLISP (which works under any operating system AutoCAD runs on) or run in the Windows' DOS compatibility box. ADS applications written for DOS do not work under Windows. This chapter describes helpful applications that work with AutoCAD Release 12 for Windows.

Executive Summary

Commercial add-on software make you more productive with AutoCAD for Windows. Here are six products, ranging in price from $25 to $195 that work with Release 11 and 12:

SirlinView/SE for Windows
- Displays DWG, DXF and HPGL files
- Redlining of drawings
- Converts displayed file to DWG and DXF format
- Copies displayed file to Clipboard in BMP and WMF format

AutoManager Classic for Windows
- Displays DWG, DXF and ICO files
- Displays more than one drawing at a time
- BaseLISP programs DDE functions
- Loads drawings, blocks, and xrefs into AutoCAD
- Copies displayed file to Clipboard in BMP and WMF format

FONTasm!
- Converts PostScript and TrueType fonts into AutoCAD and Generic CADD format
- Writes SHP source code and SHX compiled font files for AutoCAD and AutoSketch; writes FNT font files for Generic CADD
- Allows five densities of filled fonts

AutoIcon
- Multiple icon-based floating toolboxes
- Toolboxes can be grouped into workspaces
- Includes 237 BMP icons and icon editor

FloChart
- Semi-automatic creation of flow charts of unlimited size
- Uses any AutoCAD text font and any shape for elements
- AutoLISP-based application

Squiggle
- Humanizes AutoCAD drawings by applying random effects
- Reads and writes HPGL and HPGL/2 plot files
- Includes utility to send plot file to HPGL-compatible plotter attached to any communications port

SirlinView/SE for Windows

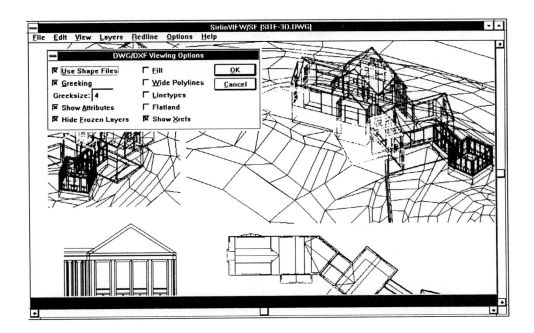

Sirlin Computer Corp.
25 Orchard View Drive
Suite 14
Londonderry, NH 03053

SirlinView/SE is a Windows program that displays DWG, DXF, and HPGL files independently of AutoCAD. Once the drawing is loaded into SirlinView, you zoom and pan about the drawing, view 3D models from different viewpoints, and switch between model and paper space. You can selectively view individual layers; the Invert command reverse the display of layers.

The redlining feature lets you mark up the drawing with lines, rectangles, circles, text, and leader-type notes. Redlines are saved on a layer named "Redline" in a separate DWG file; by default, SirlinView saves the redline drawing in the subdirectory \Acadwin\Redline.

After loading the DWG, DXF, or HPGL file, you can save it in DWG or DXF format. That makes SirlinView a drawing translator, letting you bring import into AutoCAD HP plot files and DXF files from other graphics packages.

You copy all or portions of the drawing to the Clipboard in BMP bitmap or WMF metafile format; WMF images can be imported into AutoCAD with the Paste command.

Being a Windows application, SirlinView lets you print the drawing to the system printer. Like AutoCAD, SirlinView lets you specify the size and origin of the printout. That lets you print more than one drawing per page. Unlike AutoCAD, SirlinView has options for printing a title and border around the drawing.

SirlinView lacks the programming links with AutoCAD, the ability to display more than one drawing at a time and to display individual blocks.

SirlinView runs under Windows and works with any DWG and DXF file created from AutoCAD version 2.5 through Release 12, as well as any version of HPGL.

Drawing Viewer
AutoManager Classic for Windows

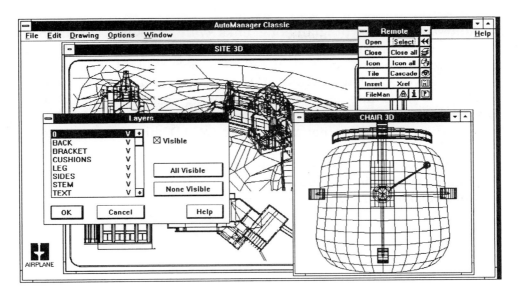

Cyco Software
1908 Cliff Valley Way
Suite 2000
Atlanta, GA 30329

AutoManager is a Windows application that displays DWG, DXF, and ICO (icon bitmaps) independently of AutoCAD. AutoManager is MDI compliant, letting you load more than one drawing, each in its own window (see Figure). Iconized files display a raster bitmap of the drawing. Once drawings are loaded into AutoManager, you zoom and pan about the drawing, view 3D models from different viewpoints, and switch between model and paper space. You can selectively view individual layers, named views, and blocks. When you select a block to view, AutoManager displays the block at all of its inserted locations.

You copy all or portions of the drawing to the Clipboard in BMP bitmap or WMF metafile format; WMF images can be imported into AutoCAD with the Paste command. The Monochrome option draws all vectors in white on the black background; there is no provision for black vectors on white background.

AutoManager has programming links with AutoCAD via DDE. It includes "Remote," a sample DDE app that controls AutoManager from an independent, floating control panel. Through AutoManager's DDE connection, you can launch AutoCAD with the current drawing, or insert blocks and xrefs into an AutoCAD drawing. AutoManager includes BaseLISP, a programming language for creating your own DDE control strings; BaseLISP does not include AutoCAD functions unique to AutoLISP.

AutoManager Classic lacks the ability to read HPGL files, save files in other formats, print the drawing or redline the drawing.

AutoManager runs under Windows and works with any DWG and DXF file created from AutoCAD 2.5 through Release 12.

Font Translator
FONTasm!

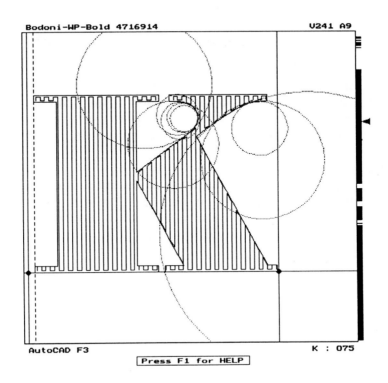

G. Gibson & Associates
Suite 201
2020 West Second Avenue
Vancouver, BC V6J 1J4

FONTasm is a DOS application that translates PostScript and TrueType font files into AutoCAD (SHP source code and SHX compiled font files) and Generic CADD v6 FNT font files. FONTasm fixes the bug in the first two releases of AutoCAD Release 12 that converted PostScript fonts to the incorrect height—about 30% too small.

Once you load a font file into FONTasm, you view each individual character in four modes: outline, filled, PostScript, and AutoCAD. The PostScript mode shows the path element control information and the declarative hint system. The AutoCAD mode shows the circular arcs and straight-line segments defining the font (see Figure). You cannot edit the font shapes with FONTasm.

Like AutoCAD's Compile command, FONTasm converts a PostScript PFB file into an AutoCAD SHX file, which is then loaded into AutoCAD with the Style command. Unlike AutoCAD, FONTasm creates SHX files that can be filled; there are five fill densities. In addition, FONTasm optionally creates the SHP source code.

The FONTasm package includes Fa.Lsp, an AutoLISP routine that creates a reference table in AutoCAD of the entire font character set.

FontASM works with any version of AutoCAD from 2.0 through to Release 12, under DOS and Windows. To work properly under Windows, use the -g3 command-line switch to force VGA mode.

IconTOOL for AutoCAD Windows

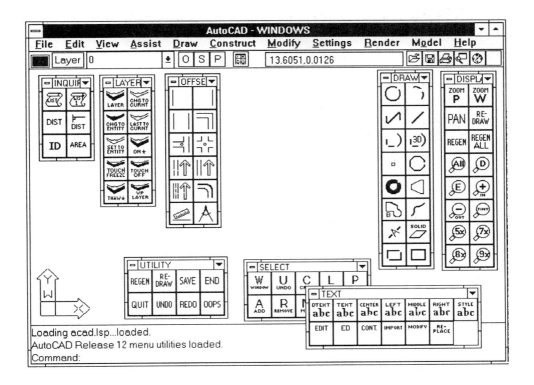

Robert McNeel & Associates
3670 Woodland Avenue North
Seattle, WA 98103

IconTOOL is a Windows add-on to AutoCAD. Whereas AutoCAD Release 12 for Windows comes with a single floating icon menu (the Toolbox), IconTOOL lets you have numerous icon menus. As in AutoCAD, clicking on an icon button sends a command or AutoLISP expression to AutoCAD. You can interactively move, resize, minimize, and add IconTOOL toolboxes, however, unlike AutoCAD.

In addition, IconTOOL provides workspaces to group toolboxes together, lets you create your own icon designs, and includes productivity routines.

The control window manages the workspaces and toolboxes. A workspace defines which toolboxes are open and their screen positions. Each toolbox has a menu button that lets you move and minimize the toolbox. Even when toolboxes are minimized their icon continues to float on top of AutoCAD.

The customization program lets you create new toolboxes and edit existing toolboxes. For each button in a toolbox, you specify an icon, a description, and the code. You can type in your own code (up to 256 characters) or paste code from a Windows text editor.

For icons, you use one of the 237 icons supplied with the package, use any other BMP file of suitable size (24 x 24 pixels, 16 colors) or create one with the Bitmap Editor included with the IconTOOL package.

IconTOOL works with AutoCAD for Windows, Releases 11 and 12.

Charting Add-on
FloChart

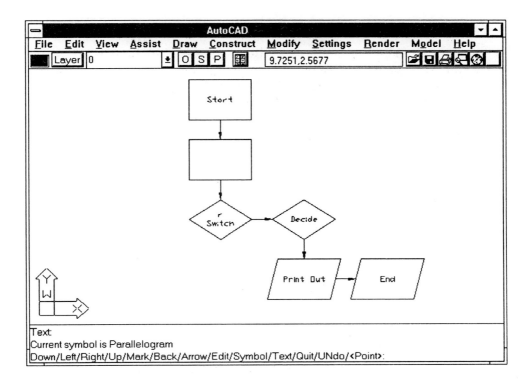

Three Sigma
P.O. Box 11
Hope, RI 02831-0011

FloChart is an AutoLISP application for creating flow charts within AutoCAD. FloChart takes care of the spacing and sizing of all flow chart elements. Since it works within AutoCAD, you can create flow charts of unlimited size.

You work with rectangles, parallelograms, diamonds and ovals; or, you can create your own symbols as DWG files. Each time you place a symbol, FloChart prompts you for one or more lines of text. You can use any AutoCAD font for the text, including converted PostScript fonts.

Arrows are automatically drawn between symbols; arrows can be labelled. When symbols branch, you place a marker then back up to the marker to work the other branch.

To change colors or linetypes, use the Change command after creating the flowchart.

FloChart works with AutoCAD Releases 10, 11, and 12 running on any operating system, including Windows.

Squiggle

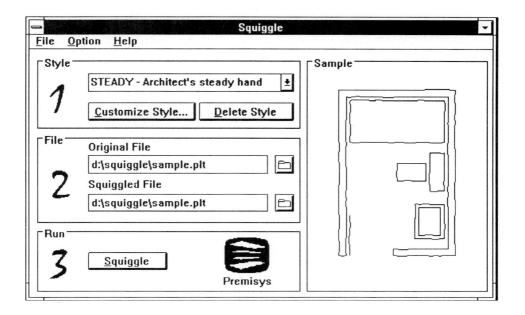

Premisys Corp
P.O. Box 10042
Chicago, IL 60610

Squiggle is a Windows application that "humanizes" the absolutely straight lines of CAD drawings. Squiggle reads HPGL and HPGL/2 plot files, then lets you select one of eight treatments: dashed, fuzzy, napkin, sketch, shaky, steady, and wavy. Squiggle rewrites the HPGL file with the biases; Squiggle does not work with WMF files.

Squiggle works best with sparse drawings; dense drawings become meaningless. How text is affected depends on the source. Some applications, such as AutoCAD, vectorize the text—this text gets squiggled. Other applications, such as Windows, specify HPGL fonts—this text is not squiggled.

You can create custom styles or fine-tune the supplied styles. Squiggle provides six actions: bend, slide, sputter, thicken, tilt, and wiggle. Each action has one or two parameters associated with it. For example, When Squiggle bends a line, you can specify the maximum rise and fall of the bend.

The Squiggle package includes a command-line version (meant for DOS and batch conversions) and a utility that sends the plot file to an HPGL-compatible plotter attached to any serial and parallel port.

Squiggle works with any software package that can output an HPGL plot file to disk, including AutoCAD Release 12 for Windows.

Windows Shareware

I nterest in shareware programs has increased as better programming tools make hotshot application design effortless. Several shareware applications have been written specific to AutoCAD and there are dozens of shareware and freeware programs available that make it easier to use Windows itself. Here we look at eight low-cost utilities that display and convert graphic files, organize your work, and tell you about your computer's Windows system.

Executive Summary

These eight programs are available on the bonus diskette (see back of book for ordering details) or from data libraries in CompuServe's advanced Windows forum (GO WINADV) and AutoCAD forum (GO ACAD).

LoadMon by Lantern Corp
- Displays CPU load, GDI, and memory consumption
- Updates every one second; 30-second history

Graphic Viewer by M. Nordan
- Displays all Windows-standard graphic formats: BMP, ICO, RLE, and WMF files
- Converts BMP and RLE into each other's format

Graphic Workshop by Alchemy Mindworks
- Converts between 13 formats: BMP, CUT, GIF, IMG, LBM, MAC, MSP, PCX, PIC, RLE, TGA, TIFF, and WPG
- Converts text files into graphics formats
- Creates EXE file that allows standalone viewing of graphic file

PixFolio by Alan Kempe
- Converts between 19 formats: IFF, FLI, FLC, CEL, GIF, EPS, GEM, IMG, MAC, DRW, PCX, RLE, TGA, TIFF, BMP, CLP, ICN, WMF, and WPG
- Catalogs images for display and print out

Bmp2Dxf by Stan Katz
- Converts a BMP file into DXF format
- Raster dots converted into horizontal polylines on layer BMP

TaskTracker by Marquette Computer Consultants
- Keeps a log of the time spent in Windows applications
- Logs phone calls when used with Windows Terminal
- Outputs reports in Excel, Word and CDF formats

Lister by Workgroup Systems
- Lists all EXE, DRV, FON, and DLL files loaded by Windows
- Lists loads in order, and number of times accessed

WinDump by John Napier
- Windows-based file display and hex editor of files up to 2GB in size
- MDI-compliant; compares two files for differences

What is Shareware?

There is no shortage of good software available for AutoCAD and Windows users at reasonable prices. Called "shareware," you obtain the software for free or at some nominal cost. Try the software and if you find yourself using it, pay the programmer the asking price—usually in the range of $5 to $50.

Few shareware programmers become wealthy; estimates range from 1% to 10% of shareware users ever pay the registration fee. When you send the programmer the asking price, you become a registered owner. In return, you *may* receive the most recent version of the software, more thorough documentation, telephone support and/or bonus software.

Shareware is a form of software marketing; it isn't free software. Shareware is a grass-roots method of software distribution; the software is distributed by passing copies on to others by disk or bulletin board. It allows users to risk the time it takes to discover whether a new piece of software is useful without risking the purchase price.

Shareware software has become a large enough business to warrant its own a professional association. The Association of Shareware Professionals makes sure that the shareware principle works for you. If you've paid for the software and you have problems but can't come to an agreement with the programmer, ASP may be able to help. The ASP Ombudsman helps resolve disputes with ASP members; it does not provide technical support. For more information, contact ASP at PO Box 5786, Bellevue WA 98006 or via CompuServe on 70007,3536.

Freeware and Public Domain Software. In addition to shareware, there are two other forms of software distribution: freeware and software placed in the public domain.

Freeware, unlike shareware, is free. You can use it without needing to compensate the programmer. The freeware programmer retains the copyright on the software; however, freeware often includes the source code, which you can make use of in your own programming projects.

When software placed in the public domain, the programmers gives up their copyright on the code. Like freeware, public domain software is free.

I downloaded these utilities from CompuServe's Autodesk and Windows forums. If you don't have access to CompuServe, the software is also available directly from the programmer and on the bonus diskette; your local user group may have some of these programs in their software library.

Some of these programs require the Visual Basic runtime module, Vbrun100.Dll or Vbrun200.Dll, to run. These dynamic link libraries are included with AutoCAD for Windows.

CPU Monitor
LoadMon

Lantern, Corp
Edward Hutchins
CIS 73650,375

Nearly a decade ago, I babysat a Sun 3 workstation for a weekend. On its screen, it had a little CPU monitor that showed a line chart—in real-time—how hard the Motorola 68020 chip had been working for the previous 60 seconds. Ever since then, I've always wanted one for my Windows system.

Edward Hutchins created exactly what I've been wanting. LoadMon (freeware; short for load monitor) is an icon-size application that displays the CPU load in real time as a bar chart (see Figure, above). The display is updated every second and shows the history of the previous 30 seconds of CPU activity.

The icon displays two lines. The green line (lower down) is either the GDI (graphical device interface) memory or the User Library Data segment—whichever is less. The maximum amount of memory allocated to these is 64 KB.

The red line (near the top) represents the available global memory. That is usually the net amount of: the RAM memory plus the virtual memory minus the memory being used. A typical computer with 8 MB of RAM also has 8 MB virtual memory.

Clicking on the icon and selecting the **About** button lists these statistics in actual values (MB, KB, etc) and in percentages.

You'll find that disk accesses use 100% of the CPU workload, while mouse movement takes up small blips of processing load. Interprocess communication, such as DDE and OLE, imposes a 50% load on the CPU. I've found LoadMon useful for alerting me of a locked up application; in these cases, the CPU load shows a steady one-third to one-half load, even when nothing else appears to be happening.

Graphic Viewer

M. Nordan
122 Overbrook Drive
Concord, NC 28025
CIS 76535,1421

As a *graphical* user interface, Windows encourages you to dabble in graphics far more than plain old DOS. Two commands in AutoCAD for Windows export images in Windows' formats: the **Copy Image** menu item creates a BMP bitmap raster file, while the **Copy Vectors** command creates a WMF vector metafile.

Graphic Viewer (freeware) is a file viewer that displays graphics files saved in Windows' four graphics formats:

- BMP raster bitmap files
- RLE compressed bitmap files
- ICO raster icon files
- WMF vector metafiles

To view a graphics file, you either load a file with **Open File**, or use the **Paste** menu item to load the current image from the Clipboard (see Figure). Once loaded in Graphic Viewer, you can use the **Copy** command to copy the current image to the Clipboard.

Or, you can save BMP and RLE files in each other's formats; programmer M. Nordan apologizes that ICO and WMF files cannot be converted. Graphic Viewer requires VBRun100.Dll.

TIP NUMBER 27
Automatic Startup

On my system, I make Windows automatically load several of these utilities, including LoadMon and Clock. If your computer uses version 3.0, add the following line to the [Windows] section of the Win.Ini file:

```
[Windows]
load=loadmon.exe
load=clock.exe
```

If your system runs Windows v3.1 or Windows for Workgroups, drag the programs' icons to the Startup group. ■

Graphic Workshop

```
╔══════════════════ Graphic Workshop ══════════════════ ▼ ╗
║ Convert │ Crop │ Dither │ Effects │ Get info │ Help │ Print │ Reverse │ Scale ║
║ Trnsfrm │ View │ Clear all │ Tag all │ Rename │ Delete │ Setup │ About │ Quit ║
╟──────────────────────────────────────────────────────────╢
║  Files in:  c:\pcx                                        ║
║                              ┌─── Destination ───┐        ║
║  acadlogo.tif   nexus.tif    │  MAC   │   TGA    │        ║
║  alta256.pcx    npuck.pcx    ├────────┼──────────┤        ║
║  artist64.pcx   pencilc.pcx  │  IMG   │   CUT    │        ║
║  bfyfish1.tga   pencilc2.pcx ├────────┼──────────┤        ║
║  bldg.tif       puck64.pcx   │  PCX   │   BMP    │        ║
║  bnc64.pcx      rose.pcx     ├────────┼──────────┤        ║
║  brick.bmp      tallbldg.tif │  GIF   │   MSP    │        ║
║  buttons.pcx    timexc.pcx   ├────────┼──────────┤        ║
║  cable64.pcx    x_alta25.tga │  TIF   │   LBM    │        ║
║  cablesc.pcx    [..]         ├────────┼──────────┤        ║
║  cadvance.tif   [-a-]        │  WPG   │   EXE    │        ║
║  disk64.pcx     [-b-]        ├────────┼──────────┤        ║
║  divider.pcx    [-c-]        │  PIC   │   TXT    │        ║
║  fern.gif       [-d-]        ├────────┼──────────┤        ║
║  frog.gif                    │  RLE   │  Cancel  │        ║
║  imouse64.pcx                └───────────────────┘        ║
╚══════════════════════════════════════════════════════════╝
```

Alchemy Mindworks
P.O. Box 500
Beeton, ON L0G 1A6

Graphic Workshop ($40; shareware) is a Windows program that performs quick conversions between 13 formats: BMP, CUT, GIF, IMG, LBM, MAC, MSP, PCX, PIC, RLE, TGA, TIFF, and WPG. That lets you import images from AutoCAD in BMP format and translate them into other formats. In addition, Graphic Workshop convert texts files into graphics format and compresses graphic files into stand-along executable with a built-in viewer.

Graphic Workshop performs a limited number of special effects. The software includes filters to soften, sharpen, smudge, posterize, and dither the image. You can rotate the image in 90-degree increments, mirror, resize, and rescale the image. In printing, you specify sizes of 100 through 400 percent enlargement.

PixFolio

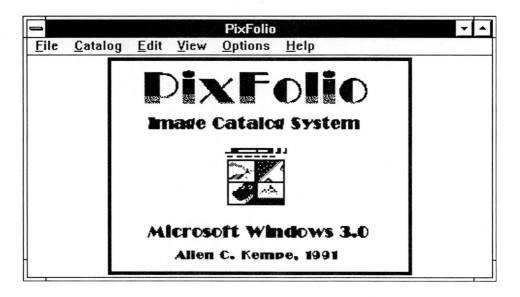

Alan Kempe
298 West Audubon Drive
Shepherdsville, KY 40165-8836
CIS 71220,23

PixFolio (shareware) is a Windows program that catalogs graphic images. AutoCAD for Windows, for example, comes with over 80 bitmap icon files. A catalog program, such as PixFolio, creates a catalog of images, which you can then quickly view or print. When printed, PixFolio prints three images per page, with full information about each image (size, format, location on disk, etc).

PixFolio performs format conversions between IFF, FLI, FLC, CEL, GIF, EPS, GEM, IMG, MAC, DRW, PCX, RLE, TGA, TIFF, BMP, CLP, ICN, WMF, and WPG. PixFolio is unique in that it can display animations created by Autodesk products, such as Animator. You can copy the image to the Clipboard and print the image. PixFolio does not perform transformations (other than resizing) or special effects.

File Conversion
Bmp2Dxf

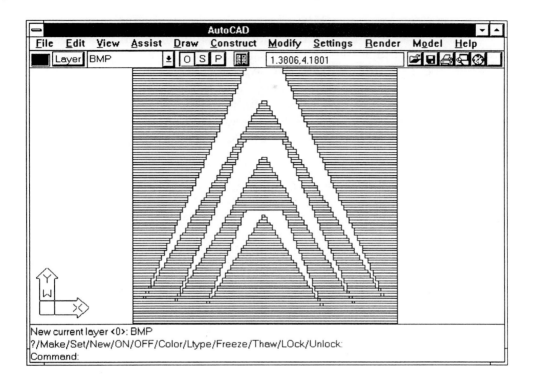

Stan Katz
P.O. Box 7242
Penndel, PA 19047-7242

BmpDxf ($25; shareware) is a DOS program that converts BMP bitmap files into a DXF file, which can be read by AutoCAD and many other graphical programs.

The program is limited to reading monochrome BMP files with a resolution of no more than 640x480. To ensure these constraints are met, create a new file with Microsoft Paintbrush, set the image attributes to 640x480 pels and black-white. Then paste the image from the Clipboard. Use the **File | Save As** command to save the file as a monochrome BMP file. Finally, you are ready to use Bmp2Dxf.

Bmp2Dxf asks you for the BMP and DXF filenames, then creates the DXF file in a minute or two to, depending on the speed of your computer.

When the DXF file is read into AutoCAD, you find it consists of horizontal polylines on layer BMP (see Figure). The polylines approximate continuous runs of black pixels in the bitmap image.

Bmp2Dxf is an effective way to import logos and small pieces of art into AutoCAD's vector format. It is not suitable to converting paper drawings to vector.

Task Tracker

```
┌──────────────────────────────────────────────────────────────────┐
│ ▬              TaskTracker: [SAMPLE.TSK]                    ▼ ▲     │
├──────────────────────────────────────────────────────────────────┤
│ File   Run   Options   Help                                        │
├──────────────────────────────────────────────────────────────────┤
│ Task 2 of 6 tasks                          10 May 1993  11:10:36   │
│ Timer OFF                              Time This Task:   05:00:00   │
│ Current Task:  │Task with elapsed time                        │ ± │
│ Task Description                                                    │
│ ┌──────────────────────────────────────────────────────────┐ ▲   │
│ │This is the second task in sample.tsk.  As you can see, five hours have passed│
│ │for this task.                                              │     │
│ │                                                            │ ▼   │
│ └──────────────────────────────────────────────────────────┘     │
│  ┌─ Task Controls ──────────────────────────────────┐             │
│  │  ┌──────────┐  ┌──────────┐  ┌───────────┐        │             │
│  │  │Start Timer│  │Add Task  │  │Edit Name  │        │             │
│  │  └──────────┘  └──────────┘  └───────────┘        │             │
│  │  ┌──────────┐  ┌──────────┐  ┌───────────┐        │             │
│  │  │Reset Time │  │Delete Task│  │Edit Time  │        │             │
│  │  └──────────┘  └──────────┘  └───────────┘        │             │
│  └──────────────────────────────────────────────────┘             │
└──────────────────────────────────────────────────────────────────┘
```

Marquette Computer Consultants
Barry Seymour
22 Sirard Lane
San Rafael, CA 94901
CIS 70413,3405

TaskTracker keeps track of the time you spend in Windows applications, such as AutoCAD for Windows (see Figure, above). The program allows you to define tasks for a project and keeps track of the time you spend on those tasks. For example, TaskTracker keeps track of the time you spend on phone calls via the dialer applet, Terminal, included with Windows.

TaskTracker then generates accurate billing records. Tasks are grouped by project file and can be defined by software, by project or by client. Project files are text files editable by the Windows Notepad text editor.

To add up the billable hours, TaskTracker exports data to the Microsoft Excel for Windows spreadsheet, Windows Write or Microsoft Word for Windows word processors. To create the invoices, TaskTracker outputs its information in tab-delimited format any word processor.

A number of features automate the time tracking process. AutoStart automatically stops and resets the timer when you switch tasks. AutoSave records the tracking information to disk at user-defined intervals. Task spawning lets you re-use time billing forms for new clients. Applets gives you quick access to the applications bundled in with Windows, such as Write and Cardfile. TaskTracker requires VBRun100.Ddl.

System Checker
Lister

Uses	Date/Time	Size	Filename
56	10/01/92 03:11 am	75490	D:\WINDOWS\SYSTEM\KRNL386.EXE
43	10/01/92 03:11 am	2304	D:\WINDOWS\SYSTEM\SYSTEM.DRV
43	10/01/92 03:11 am	7568	D:\WINDOWS\SYSTEM\KEYBOARD.DRV
41	10/01/92 03:11 am	10672	D:\WINDOWS\SYSTEM\MOUSE.DRV
42	04/22/92 11:51 am	83216	D:\WINDOWS\SYSTEM\ULTRABIG.DRV
41	10/01/92 03:11 am	3440	D:\WINDOWS\SYSTEM\MMSOUND.DRV
41	10/01/92 03:11 am	9632	D:\WINDOWS\SYSTEM\COMM.DRV
3	03/10/92 03:10 am	7280	D:\WINDOWS\SYSTEM\VGASYS.FON
3	03/10/92 03:10 am	5168	D:\WINDOWS\SYSTEM\VGAOEM.FON
42	10/01/92 03:11 am	220800	D:\WINDOWS\SYSTEM\GDI.EXE
2	03/10/92 03:10 am	5360	D:\WINDOWS\SYSTEM\VGAFIX.FON
40	03/17/93 09:05 am	264016	D:\WINDOWS\SYSTEM\USER.EXE
1	10/01/92 03:11 am	8704	D:\WINDOWS\SYSTEM\MODERN.FON
1	10/01/92 03:11 am	12288	D:\WINDOWS\SYSTEM\SCRIPT.FON
1	10/01/92 03:11 am	13312	D:\WINDOWS\SYSTEM\ROMAN.FON

The window title bar reads **Currently Loaded Modules** with a menu item **List**.

Workgroup Systems
Ramesh Rooplahl
CIS 72260,2637

Lister (freeware) is a Windows utility that reports on the programs used by Windows. Windows is a complex operating environment that uses many files and many different kinds of files: EXE executables, DRV drivers, FON fonts, DLL dynamic link libraries, VDX virtual device drivers, INI initialization files, and more.

Lister lists the EXE, DLL, DRV, and FON files used by the current session of Windows. It lists them in the order they were loaded and the number of times the files have been accessed.

You can have Lister list all four types of files, or each group individually. The Date/Time and Size columns refer to the files' date/time of create and file size; they do not refer to the date/time the file was loaded by Windows or the memory used by the file.

WinDump

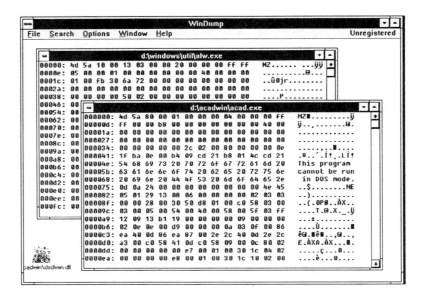

John Napier
1 Wayside Green
Woodcote, Reading RG8 0PR, England
CIS 100023,201

WinDump ($20; shareware) is a Windows hexadecimal dump program. By loading any file, you see the hexadecimal and ASCII structure of the file. If the file is corrupted, you might be able to make repairs with WinDump and save the file. WinDump works with files up to 2GB (two gigabytes = 2,047 MB) in size. You can print the hex characters but cannot copy them to the clipboard.

You can search for specific strings forwards and backwards, display text in three different fonts, and automatically update the file every user-specified interval. This lets you watch changes to a file in real-time. WinDump is MDI compliant, allowing you to open more than one file at a time. When you have two files loaded, you can use WinDump to find the differences between the two files. By default, the program looks for differences in a range of 250 characters; the value is user adjustable.

Multimedia AutoCAD

Audio Notes

utodesk supplies all the tools you need to convert static AutoCAD drawings into a multimedia extravaganza. The software tools let you create animations of wireframe 2D or shaded 3D drawings—even add sound notes to drawings. Unfortunately, Autodesk hasn't placed the pieces together in one place. Section 3 contains three chapters on multimedia, which describe tools for creating a masterpiece in sight and sound. In this chapter, tutorials show you how to add sound to AutoCAD drawings.

Executive Summary

AutoCAD for Windows is not an OLE (object linking and embedding) client. Thus, you cannot embed sound in an AutoCAD drawing using Object Packager supplied with Windows. Instead, you use the ANotes application supplied by Autodesk.

To add sound to a drawing, your computer needs six items:

▸ An internal sound board with a Windows-compatible device driver

▸ A microphone or other source of sound

▸ A pair of loudspeakers to hear the sound

▸ The Windows Multimedia Extension, included with Windows v3.1 and Windows for Workgroups

▸ The AutoCAD Audio Notes application

▸ And, of course, AutoCAD Releases 11 or 12 for Windows

Audio notes lets you insert sounds in a drawing. The sound is represented by a loudspeaker icon in the drawing. The sound is actually stored in a WAV-format file on disk, which can be accessed by any WAV-compatible sound editor.

Why Vocalize AutoCAD?

Autodesk first introduced sound notes with AutoCAD Release 11 running on the Sun SPARCstation (the computer includes a sound chip). By adding a sound card, microphone, and loudspeakers, you give an IBM-compatible personal computer the ability to record and playback audio notes in an AutoCAD drawing. Here are some reasons why you might want to vocalize AutoCAD:

- **Audio notes.** Although CAD software is great at improving your firm's design and drafting efficiency, there is no easy way to add casual notes to a CAD drawing, as with paper drawings (sometimes called "redlining"). Adding an audio note to the drawing makes it easier to leave a note by someone who isn't used to typing on the keyboard.

- **Handicap Access.** Placing notes in a drawing with sound can be easier for handicapped CAD users than with the keyboard.

- **Canned demos.** You are an AutoCAD developer demonstrating new software at a trade show. Combined with displaying SLD files in a slide show, AutoCAD orally describes the features of the new product.

- **Sound effects.** You are the product designer showing off a new baby rattle design to a marketing firm. AutoCAD plays animated rendered 3D images and with the rattle's sound (and the baby's cooing).

How Audio Notes Work

Anotes

Anotes.Exe is an ADS (AutoCAD development system) program that works only with AutoCAD for Windows. It allows you to record and playback sounds attached to any AutoCAD drawing. The sounds are your voice, a piece of music, or a sound effect. When you record an audio note, the Anotes program places a block in the drawing, then waits for you to talk into the microphone. Your voice is digitized—using the sound board's chip—then stored in a file on disk.

When you want to hear an audio note, Anotes prompts you to pick a loudspeaker icon in the AutoCAD drawing. It retrieves the digitized voice file, and plays it back using the sound board. The sound file is given the same name as the current drawing with the extension of A*xx*; "xx" is a hexadecimal number between 00 and FF (FF is 255 in decimal). Recording the first audio note in the Sample.Dwg stores it in a file with the name of Sample.A00.

You can record up to 256 different audio notes in one drawing; you can reuse the same audio note more than once in a drawing. To alert your drafter to update three details on a drawing, you record one voice note saying, "Please update this detail" and copy it twice more.

The Anotes program plays back audio notes in the drawing, lets you specify the duration of pause between notes, adjusts the record and playback volume, and deletes old audio notes.

TIP NUMBER 28
Audio Makes Big Files

Since sound takes up a lot of disk space, keep audio notes as short as possible. Each second of audio recording consumes 11 KB to 90 KB of disk space. The size depends on the sampling rate and sample size, which is how the sound board converts analog sound waves into a digital file. Most sound boards give you six sampling options:

Sound Board Sampling Options

Sampling Rate	Sample Size	Bytes per second
11.025 kHz	8 bits	11.3 KB
	16 bits	22.6 KB
22.05 kHz	8 bits	22.6 KB
	16 bits	45.1 KB
44.1 kHz	8 bits	45.1 KB
	16 bits	90.3 KB

The byte size values are shown for monophonic recording. Double the byte size when you record in stereo. Windows does not compress the sound file: the file takes up exactly the same amount of disk space whether you are recording a minute of silence or a minute of philharmonic orchestra.

The higher the sampling, the better the sound quality: 44.1 kHz is called "CD-quality" sound, since that is the rate that music CDs are recorded at (an hour's worth of music consumes 640 MB of data!). For voice notes, the 8-bit, 11 kHz rate is good enough. ∎

Software and Hardware Requirements

Once AutoCAD for Windows is set up for audio, it takes little effort to record and play back sounds. But to make it happen, your computer needs the right combination of software and hardware. Here is an overview of the six components needed:

Hardware. Your computer needs three items: (1) sound board, (2) microphone, and (3) loudspeakers (see Figure below).

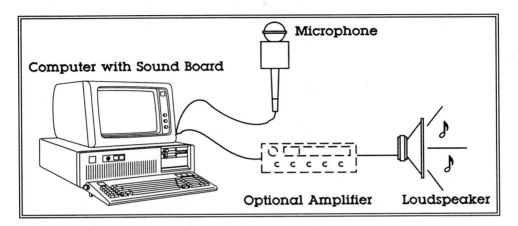

- **Sound board.** The sound board must be supported by the Microsoft Windows Multimedia Extension. Windows v3.1 and Windows for Workgroups includes the extension. The list of supported sound boards include those compatible with AdLib, Creative Labs Sound Blaster v1.0, and v1.5, Media Vision Thunder Board, Roland LAPC1, MPU-401 (most MIDI system boards), plus any board with the appropriate Windows device driver.

- **Microphone.** The microphone records voice notes or live sound effects. Any microphone will do—just check the size of the connecting plug. As alternative, you plug a cassette deck or CD player into the sound board to record short music segments or canned sound effects.

- **Loudspeaker.** The loudspeaker allows you to hear the audio notes during playback. Most sound boards include a 4 W amplifier. If the sound board does not have a built-in amplifier, it needs an external amplifier to make the sound loud enough to be heard on the speakers. To keep the playback of sound notes discrete, plug a pair of head-phones into the sound board.

```
┌─────────────────────────────────────────────────────────────┐
│  ┌───────────────────────────────────────────────────────┐  │
│  │                    TIP NUMBER 29                       │  │
│  │            Caught Without a Microphone?                │  │
│  │                                                        │  │
│  │  If you are caught without a microphone, plug the      │  │
│  │  loudspeakers (or headphones) into the Mic input and   │  │
│  │  talk into one. The sound quality is not as good as    │  │
│  │  with a microphone but it works because microphones    │  │
│  │  and loudspeakers use exactly the same technology in   │  │
│  │  reverse. ■                                            │  │
│  └───────────────────────────────────────────────────────┘  │
└─────────────────────────────────────────────────────────────┘
```

Software. The audio hardware won't do a thing until your computer is running the right software.

Your computer needs three pieces of software: (1) Windows with Multimedia Extensions; (2) AutoCAD for Windows; and (3) AutoCAD Audio Notes.

► **Windows Multimedia Extension.** If your computer is running Microsoft Windows v3.0, then you need to acquire the Multimedia Extensions. The add-on software lets Windows access sound boards and CD-ROM players.

  If you have Windows v3.1 or Windows for Workgroups, then you are in luck. These versions of Windows include the sound portion of the Multimedia Extension.

► **AutoCAD Windows Extension.** Audio does not work with any release of AutoCAD except the Windows version.

► **AutoCAD Audio Notes.** The Anotes package includes the C-language source code, a customized menu file, brief documentation, and a Windows icon.

  The Audio Notes software package is available free (except for the cost of downloading—about $3) on CompuServe's AutoCAD Forum in data library 11. Browse for file Anotes.Zip.

  If you do not have access to CompuServe, the software is also on the optional diskette (ordering information at the back of this book).

Getting Windows Ready

In preparing this book, I used the Stereo F/X sound card from ATI Technologies. The board is compatible with several sound board standards, such as Creative Labs' Sound Blaster, Ad Lib, CMS' Music, and Game Blaster Boards, and the MIDI standard (short for musical instrument device interface). The board includes an 8-watt stereo amplifier and a pair of miniloudspeakers.

Follow your sound board's installation instruction to install the board in your computer.

Configure Windows to work with the board, as follows:

1. In the Program Manager, double-click on the Control Panel icon.

2. Double-click on the Drivers icon.

3. The **Drivers** dialogue box opens, listing the names of sound drivers Windows is configured with. If you see the name compatible with your sound board (for example, the Ad Lib selection works with the ATI Stereo F/X board), select that driver.

4. If no driver is listed for your board, click on the **Add...** button to add the device driver from the floppy diskette that comes with Windows v3.1 or the sound board (see Figure).

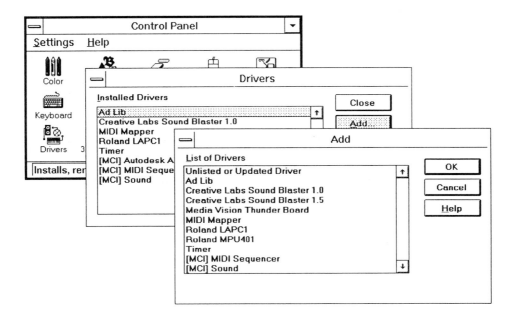

4. When you select certain drivers, the **Options...** button changes from gray to black. Click on the button to bring up a dialogue box that lets you select the interrupt and I/O (input/output) address. Windows selects default values; you should not change them unless the sound board does not work.

5. To test the sound board, go back to the Control Panel and double-click on the Sound icon. When the **Sound** dialogue box appears, click on the **Test...** button (see Figure). You should hear a sound coming from the loudspeakers.

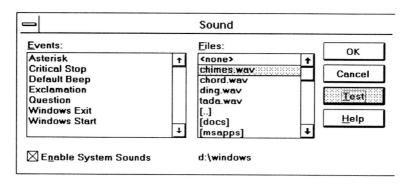

TIP NUMBER 30

Can't Afford a Sound Board?

You might not be able to afford a sound board because of the cost or because your computer has no slots free. In that case, use the PC Speaker sound driver. This driver lets Windows send sounds to the speaker built into every computer. However, the sound is awful.

Still, the PC Speaker driver is available on CompuServe and on the optional diskette available with this book. ■

Getting AutoCAD Ready

With Windows setup for sound, you now prepare AutoCAD, as follows:

1. Copy the Anotes software into the \Acadwin\Ads subdirectory. The only two files AutoCAD must have are Anotes.Exe and Anotes.Mnu.

2. Load AutoCAD for Windows and open a drawing you want to experiment on.

3. Use the Menu command to load the Anotes.Mnu menu file, as follows:

```
Command: menu
Menu file name or . for none <acad>: anotes
```

4. You load the Anotes.Exe program in one of two ways. Pick the **Audio** item from the menu bar, then select the **Load Audio Notes Program** item. AutoCAD reports:

```
Loading Audio Notes...
```

The alternate method is to drag the Anotes.Exe filename from the File Manager into the AutoCAD drawing editor.

When you select **Audio**, the pop-down menu displays the following choices:

Audio

New Note	▸ Insert a new audio note
Rerecord	▸ Change an existing audio note
Append	▸ Add to an existing audio note
Play	▸ Select an audio note to play
Multiple Play	▸ Play a selection of audio notes
List	▸ List information about an audio note
Status	▸ Report the status of all audio notes
Purge	▸ Purge one or more audio notes
Audio Variables	
Volume	▸ Change the record and playback volume
Scale	▸ Change the insertion scale of the block
Pause	▸ Pause between multiple audio note playback
Window	▸ Define audio note selection

Audio Notes Commands

Anotes has the following 13 commands to handle audio notes:

Commands in ANotes.Exe

Command	Short Form	Function
AudioNote	Anote	Primary Anote command; options are: ‣ New note: create new audio note ‣ Rerecord: change audio note ‣ Append: add to audio note ‣ Play: play an audio note ‣ Multiple-play: play several audio notes
AudioPlay	Aplay	Play a selected audio note
AudioPlayM	Aplaym	Play a selection set of audio notes
AudioStatus	Astatus	Report on all audio notes in the drawing
AudioPurge	Apurge	Erase old sound notes and associated files
AudioList	Alist	List information about a selected audio note
AudioVars	Avars	List of audio note variables
AudioPause	Apause	Determine whether pause occurs between playback of AplayM command
AudioScale	Ascale	Insertion scale of loudspeaker block
AudioVolume	Avolume	Controls volume of record and playback on a scale of 0 to 100
AudioWindow	Awindow	Determines search criterion for Asearch command
AudioVersion	Aversion	Displays version number of Anotes

You type in the full-length or short-form version of each command. Two commands were documented but not implemented in Anotes.Exe v1.0: AudioOutput and AudioSearch.

Tutorial 1
Recording Sound Notes

With Windows and AutoCAD wired for sound, let's try recording and playing audio notes.

1. Select the **Audio | New Note** command. Anote prints the following on the text screen, which you can ignore:

   ```
   Command: Audionote
   Rerecord/Play/Multiple-play/Append/<New Note>:
   ```

2. Anote prompts you to pick a point in the drawing where you want the audio note located, as follows:

   ```
   Insertion point of Audio Note: <pick a point>
   ```

3. Anote inserts the loudspeaker block, then displays the **Anotes Message** dialogue box (see Figure, next page).
   If you pick **No**, the command is canceled.
   When you pick **Yes**, Anotes begins recording, prompting you with the following message:

   ```
   Recording Started. Any key to stop.
   ```

TIP NUMBER 31
AutoCAD Can't Find Anotes

If AutoCAD doesn't find Anotes, it reports the error message:

```
ERROR: File not found.
Unable to load Audio Notes executable.
```

In this case, load the program by the manual method, as follows:

```
Command: (xload "\\acadwin\\ads\\anotes")
"\\acadwin\\ads\\anotes"
```

■

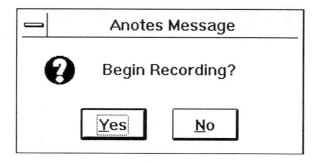

Anotes Message

Begin Recording?

Yes   No

4. Speak a short message into the microphone, such as "Confirm the door's model number with client."

5. Press a mouse button or a keyboard key to tell Anotes that you have finished recording. Anotes reports the duration of the sound note as follows:

```
Done recording. Audio Note saved (3.9 sec).
```

Since each note takes up about 11 KB of disk space, you can quickly calculate that this note took about 43 KB. The sound is stored on disk in a file named *drawing.A00*.

6. To hear yourself speak from the AutoCAD drawing, select **Audio | Play** from the menu, or type the **AudioPlay** command, as follows:

```
Command: audioplay
Select Audio Note to play: <pick the speaker block>
```

Anote plays back the audio note "...confirm the door's model number with client..."

7. To list information about the audio note, select **Audio | List** from the menu or type in the **AudioList** command, as follows:

```
Command: audiolist
Select Audio Note to list: <pick speaker block>
    Audio Note Index:  0
    Insertion Point:   2150, 4550, 0
    Recording User:    WINDOWS
    Recording Date:    19940331.1501
    Note Length:       3.9 seconds
    Note File Size:    42K bytes
```

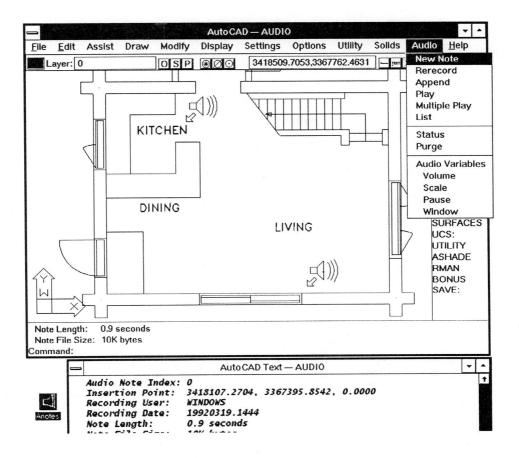

AutoCAD displays the information on the text screen; if necessary, press <F2> to see to the text screen. The Audio Note Index refers to the incremental note number—the first note is index 0.

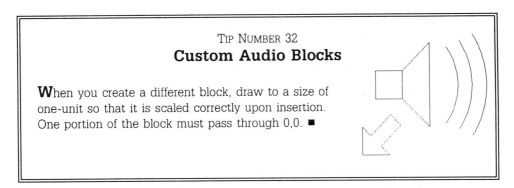

TIP NUMBER 32
Custom Audio Blocks

When you create a different block, draw to a size of one-unit so that it is scaled correctly upon insertion. One portion of the block must pass through 0,0. ■

Customizing Audio Notes

Here are a number of ideas for customizing the audio notes application:

Loudspeaker block. The block is a drawing of a loudspeaker and an arrow, called "Audio_Note." You define your own block for different kinds of audio notes. For example, you can customize blocks with each person's initials in them or a symbol describing the kind of audio note.

WAV file playback. Audio notes are stored in Microsoft's WAV (short for waveform) audio file format. You can play the audio note files with any other software that plays WAV-format files by just renaming the extension from Axx to WAV.

Media Player, included with Windows v3.1, plays WAV sound files (with the WAV extension) and MIDI files (with MID and RMI extensions) along with compact disks and video disk players (see Figure).

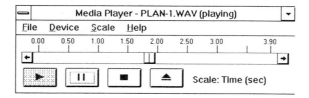

Sound Recorder is the more interesting of the two programs, although it only reads WAV files. While playing back the audio note, Sound Recorder displays the waveform in real time (see Figure). Edit the audio note by reversing the sound, adding an echo, speeding up or slowing down, changing the volume, and inserting other WAV files. As the name implies, Sound Recorder records, just as Audio Notes does. Replay the edited WAV file in AutoCAD by renaming the extension to Axx.

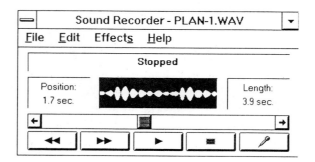

10

Animating AutoCAD

In 1987, Autodesk first dipped its corporate toe into animation when it released AutoFlix. Displaying grainy images at 320 x 175 resolution (EGA resolution quartered by dithering to display more than 16 colors), AutoFlix amazed PC users by playing back movie files at speeds of up to 12 frames per second. Since then, resolution, colors, and playback speeds of PC-based movies have greatly improved. In the last chapter, you saw how to add audio notes to AutoCAD drawings. The second part to the multimedia equation is animation. In this chapter, you find out how to animate AutoCAD 3D drawings.

Executive Summary

With the Automation Tool Kit, you can create three types of animations from 3D AutoCAD drawings:

▸ **Path Animation:** you walk and fly through the 3D model.

▸ **Kinetic Animation:** the parts of the 3D model move.

▸ **General Animation:** you walk and fly through the 3D model while parts of the model also move.

To create an animation from an AutoCAD drawing takes these four steps:

1. **Preparation in AutoCAD:** define the camera parameters, define the motion paths and check the camera aim.

2. **Processing by AutoShade:** Render each frame, one at a time.

3. **Compiling via FliMaker:** Combine the individual frame files into a single movie file.

4. **Playback with AaPlay:** Playback and view the movie.

This chapter covers the first three steps; the next chapter describes step 4.

Why Animate AutoCAD?

Here are some ways to animate AutoCAD drawings:

▸ **Impact Studies.** An engineering firm is designing a new bridge for the state highways department. To show residents the impact of the bridge approach, the firm creates a "drive-through" animation from an AutoCAD drawing of the district's land contour maps.

▸ **Clearance Checking.** A window manufacturer designs a new opener for wood and aluminum windows. To determine the clearance, the firm's designers animate their AutoCAD drawing.

▸ **Project Presentations.** An architectural firm is bidding for the design of a new church building. The firm creates an animated "walk-through" of the sanctuary with opening doors. The animation is based on preliminary concept drawings created in AutoCAD.

It's worthwhile to animate an AutoCAD drawing if the process saves you money later in the building process. For the engineering firm, getting early approval eliminates costly changes that crop up later in the design cycle. For the window manufacturer, computerized animation reduces the cost of building prototypes of the window opener. For the architectural firm, the walk-though may help win the contract.

Three Kinds of Animation

The examples categorize animations: path, kinetic, and general.

▸ **Path Animation.** The bridge route fly-through is an example of path animation. The camera move along a path through the drawing, while the drawing parts remain fixed in place

▸ **Kinetic Animation.** The window opener is an example of kinetic animation. The drawing parts move (kinetics), while the camera remains fixed in place

▸ **General Animation.** The architectural walk-through is an example of general animation. Both the camera and the parts move in the drawing—the completely general case of animation.

Of the three types of animations, the path animation is the easiest to generate; the kinetic animation is the most difficult.

Four Steps to Animation

No matter which type of animation you create, you go through three steps to animate an AutoCAD drawing:

1. **Preparation.** In AutoCAD, you prepare the 3D drawing for animation by setting the camera (and, optionally, the lights), defining the path of motion, and ensuring that the camera is aimed correctly.

2. **Processing.** In AutoShade, you render each frame—one-by-one. (You cannot use Release 12's AVE Render module, since Autodesk chose not to update the Animation Tool Kit.)

3. **Compiling.** In FliMaker, the individual frames are compiled into a single movie file.

4. **Playback.** In AaPlay, the movie is played back (see Chapter 11).

If you want to create an animation of a wireframe drawing, then you skip step 2, processing with AutoShade. Wireframe is the only way to animate a 2D drawing since AutoShade does not shade objects with no thickness.

Hardware and Software Requirements

Before beginning the tutorials in this chapter, you gather together the software and hardware needed to create an animation. Preparing an animation takes significant hardware—much more than audio notes do.

Although you may want experiment with animation on a slower machine, a 486 or Pentium with 16 MB of memory, and many megabytes of free disk space is required for production use.

A FLM filmroll file is created for each frame of a kinetic animation. One hundred frames use 5 MB of disk space in FLM files, another 5 MB in RND rendering files, and 0.25 MB to 0.75 MB for the final movie file. (Once you are satisfied with the movie, you erase the FLM and RND files.) In the meantime, you've used up 10 MB of disk space for an animation that runs for... oh, about seven seconds.

The time required to process a single frame—from AutoCAD through rendering to compiling—takes as long as 30 seconds. The time depends on the complexity of the image and the speed of the computer. The seven-second movie mentioned above takes nearly an hour of processing time. Since most steps are automated, the bulk of the time is spent in CPU processing time; the faster the computer, the shorter the time to completion.

Bill Gates once noted that animation software makes the greatest demand on computer hardware. If you decide to add photo-realism with another product such as RenderMan, the hardware demands increase exponentially. Rendering a single frame with RenderMan takes between several minutes and several hours, once again depending on the complexity and the CPU. Targa-format files consume 0.5 MB per frame. That 100-frame seven-second movie now needs 100 MB free disk space during processing.

AutoCAD for Windows comes with many (but not all) of the software utilities needed to create rendered animations. Missing is the Animation Tool Kit, a collection of AutoLISP routines that make it easier to create animations (the ATK is available on CIS, with AutoShade v2, and on the bonus diskette; see the back of this book for ordering details). If you want to take advantage of RenderMan's photo-realistic effects, you'll need AutoShade v2, and the utility program TgaFli (included with the ATK) converts Targa format files into VGA format. When you register Autodesk Animator Pro, you receive the Autodesk Animation Player for Windows software.

Tutorial 1
Setting Up the Drawing

This first tutorial shows you how to set up a drawing in AutoCAD for the easiest kind of animation, the path animation.

The first step is to prepare the AutoCAD drawing: create a new layer to hold the camera's path, draw the path, and run the Animation Tool Kit's AutoLISP routines.

1. Load AutoCAD for Windows and open Shuttle.Dwg, which is located in subdirectory \Acadwin\sample. As you follow along, you can use any other 3D drawing that you would like to animate.

2. The Shuttle drawing is set to paper space showing multiple viewports. You want a single viewport of the image, so turn on Tilemode, as follows:

   ```
   Command: tilemode
   New value for TILEMODE <0>: 1
   Regenerating drawing.
   ```

3. Change the UCS (user-defined coordinate system) to the plan view, as follows:

   ```
   Command: plan
   <Current UCS>/Ucs/World: world
   Regenerating drawing.
   Command: ucs
   Origin/ZAxis/3point/Entity/View/X/Y/Z/Prev/Restore/
       Save/Del/?/<World>: view
   ```

4. Create the new layer called "Path" with the color of white, on which you draw the camera's path, as follows:

   ```
   Command: layer
   ?/Make/Set/New/ON/OFF/Color/Ltype/Freeze/Thaw: make
   New current layer <0>: path
   ?/Make/Set/New/ON/OFF/Color/Ltype/Freeze/Thaw: color
   Color: white
   Layer name(s) for color 4 (cyan) <PATH>: <Enter>
   ?/Make/Set/New/ON/OFF/Color/Ltype/Freeze/Thaw:
       <Enter>
   ```

5. Create lots of space around the shuttle with the Zoom command, as follows:

```
Command: zoom
All/.../<Scale(X/XP)>: 0.1x
Regenerating drawing.
```

6. Draw the path as a polyline, as the Animation Tool Kit insists it must be. But to draw a circular path, you cannot use the Circle command; use the Ellipse command instead, which draws a circle (as a polyline arc) when you specify the rotation angle of 0 degrees. However, you cannot drawing an ellipse with 3D coordinates; you have to change the working elevation, as follows:

```
Command: elev
New current elevation <0.0000>: 50
New current thickness <0.0000>: <Enter>
```

The elevation of 50' ensures the entire shuttle fills the camera's view.

7. With the elevation raised to 50 feet, now you can draw the ellipse, as follows (see Figure):

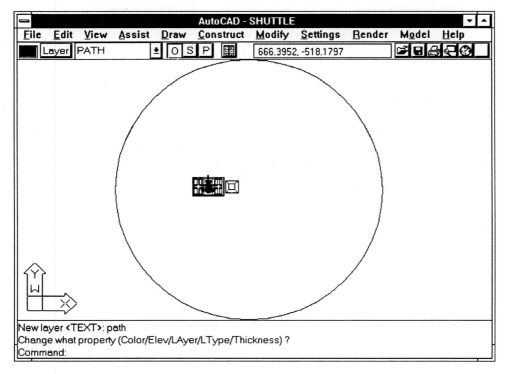

```
Command: ellipse
<Axis endpoint 1>/Center: center
Center of ellipse: 0,0
Axis endpoint: <pick at top edge of screen>
<Other axis distance>/Rotation: rotation
Rotation around major axis: 0
```

8. With the drawing prepared for animation, ensure the Animation Tool
   Kit is installed on your computer. (If you own AutoShade v2, the ATK
   is on the disks labelled "AutoFlix.") Load the ATK menu file, which
   might be called Aacad.Mnu or Ashade.Mnu (either works), as follows:

```
Command: menu
Menu file name or . for none <acad>: aacad
Loaded menu C:\ACADWIN\AACAD.mnx
```

When you click on **Utility | Animation**, the Animation menu replaces
the Utility menu. It contains the following commands:

Animation

ATK Setup...	▸ Create an ATK setup block
Edit Setup...	▸ Edit the ATK setup block
Make a camera script	▸ Create a camera script
Animate entities	▸ Animate selected entities
Animate blocks	▸ Animate selected blocks
Preview a scene	▸ Preview one or more scenes
Measure path length	▸ Measure length of the camera path
Display path numbers	▸ Display frame numbers along the path
Create point file	▸ Create a file of frame coordinates
.SLD walkthrough	▸ Create AutoCAD-rendered SLD files
Utility menu...	▸ Return to the **Utility** menu

7. Save the modified shuttle drawing with the name "ATK," as follows:

```
Command: saveas
File name <SHUTTLE>: atk
```

Tutorial 2
Creating the Filmroll

In the second tutorial, the LISP routine records the view coordinates at each of the 50 camera positions along the circular path pointed at the center of the shuttle.

1. From the **Animation** menu pick **ATK Setup...** and answer the prompts, as follows:

```
Command: <pick ATK Setup...>
Loading...
Command: atksetup
ATK Setup name: atk
ATK Setup location: <pick a location on the screen>
```

The tool kit's LISP routine inserts the ATK Setup block at the location you pick. The block consists of attributes that control the creation of the filmroll file (see Figure).

The attributes are displayed by the **Edit Attributes** dialogue box (see Figure, next page). You leave most of the values as they are; those marked with [R] apply only if you plan to use RenderMan for rendering the animation. Some attributes you may want to change are:

- **Name for ATK setup.** If you create more than one animation in this drawing, then you will want to use different names. If you create a single movie, use the drawing name (ATK, in this case) as the setup block name to eliminate confusion later.

- **Directory to place files.** Don't use the default "\ACADWIN" since the subdirectory will become cluttered by hundreds of files created during the animation process. Use the Windows File Manager to create a new subdirectory, such as "\Temp."

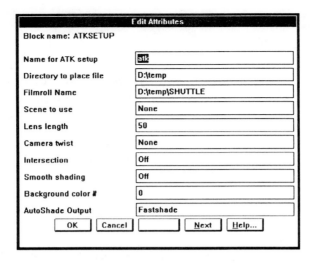

Edit Attributes

Block name: ATKSETUP

Name for ATK setup	atk
Directory to place file	D:\temp
Filmroll Name	D:\temp\SHUTTLE
Scene to use	None
Lens length	50
Camera twist	None
Intersection	Off
Smooth shading	Off
Background color #	0
AutoShade Output	Fastshade

OK   Cancel   Next   Help...

▶ **Lens length.** The default value, 30 mm, is a wide-angle lens suitable for most purposes. If you supply two values separated by a comma, the view zooms during the animation. For example, "20,70" varies the focal length from 20 mm (very wide angle) to 70 mm (moderate telephoto) over the course of the camera path. For this tutorial, leave it at 30 mm.

▶ **Camera twist.** The default value, 0, means the camera view does not twist. A numerical value means the camera view twists during animation. For example, 180 twists the view from 0 (right-side up) to 180 degrees (upside down) over the course of the camera path.

▶ **Intersection.** Changing to "Yes" means AutoShade performs intersection checking during shading. Since intersection checking takes a long time, leave this option set to "No" unless the shading turns out poorly.

▶ **Smooth shade.** Changing to "Yes" means AutoShade applies smooth shading to your 3D model. For tutorials and rough planning runs, you leave this set to "No" to save time.

▶ **AutoShade output.** Fastshade is the fastest but may make mistakes; Fullshade is slower but more accurate. For these tutorials, leave the setting at Fastshade. Do not use Quickshade, since Flimaker cannot read the shaded files created by the Quickshade process.

2. With the ATK Block set up, place the camera positions along the path. Pick **Animation | Make a camera script** to create the camera positions:

```
Command: <pick Make a camera script>
Loading... PATH v1.01 - Loaded!
Command: path
```

3. Use "ATK" as the name for the animation and the filmroll. You leave kinetic animation out of this tutorial, as follows:

```
Animation name <\Temp>: atk
Kinetic animation? <N> <Enter>
Filmroll name <\Temp>: atk
```

4. You type in any number of frames you like. A smaller number of frames take less processing time, while a larger number creates a smoother animation; 50 is a good number for the purposes of the tutorial. On my 40 MHz 386, 50 frames takes a total of about an hour to create the animation, start to finish.

```
Number of Frames: 50
```

5. Pick the default, Path, since you want the camera to travel along the ellipse path. Since the direction of the camera along the ellipse depends on how it was drawn (counterclockwise), you can have the LISP routine reverse the path.

```
Camera position: Path/Fixed/List <Path>: <Enter>
Camera path>> Select a polyline: <pick ellipse>
Reverse path direction? <N>: <Enter>
Dividing polyline and collecting points...
```

6. Pick a fixed point, such as the center of the shuttle, for the camera to look at, as follows:

```
Target position: Fixed/Path/Same path/List <Fixed>:
   <Enter>
Fixed target>> Pick a point: .xy
of <pick center of shuttle>
(need z): 50
```

The LISP routine creates the FLM filmroll file used by AutoShade:

```
Create a filmroll now? <N>: y
filmroll
```

```
Enter filmroll file name <\Temp>: C:\Temp\atk
Creating the filmroll file
Processing face: 2816
Filmroll file created.
```

The LISP routine creates the SCR script file (used by AutoShade to render the shuttle) and the MVI script file used by Flimaker to compile the rendering files into an Animator-compatible animation), as follows:

```
AutoShade script C:\Temp\atk.scr has been Created.
Animation list C:\Temp\atk.mvi has been Created.
```

Fixing Framing Problems

You have no control over the location of the first frame on a circular path; AutoCAD simply picks the starting point of the ellipse, which is at the 12-o'clock point. If you want the first frame to start somewhere else on the ellipse, use the Rotate command to rotate the ellipse about its center.

Finding Frame Numbers. If you don't know where the frame positions are located along the path, pick **Animation | Display path numbers** display the frame number, as follows (see Figure):

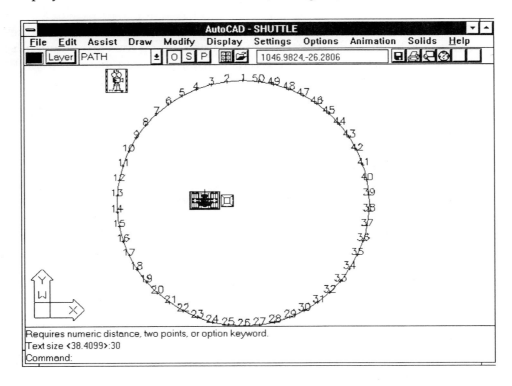

```
Command: <pick Display path numbers>
Command: ptsmark
Number of frames: 50
First path>> Pline/List <Pline>: <Enter>
Select a polyline: <pick ellipse>
Reverse path direction? <N>: <Enter>
Dividing polyline and collecting points...
Second path>> Pline/Fixed/List <none>: <Enter>
Text size <35.7108>: 30
```

Calculating the Animation Speed. If you're not sure how many frames to use, the Animation Tool Kit includes the Plength command, which calculates the distance between camera positions. Pick the **Measure path length** from the Animation menu, as follows:

```
Command: <pick Measure path length>
Command: plength
Select a polyline: <pick ellipse>
Number of frames: 50
Single segment length for 50 frames = 67.2689
Total length = 3363.45
```

Now that you know the length of the path and the distance between frames, you can work out the speed of the camera along the path if you know the animation playback speed. For a playback speed of 24 fps (frames per second), the camera speed is:

```
67.2689 feet per frame * 24 fps
= 1,614 feet per second * 3,600 second per hour
= 5,812,033 feet / 5,280 feet per mile
= 1,100 miles per hour
```

The camera appears to move at about 1,000 mph around the shuttle.

Previewing the Animation. The Animation Tool Kit includes a command that lets you preview the animation within AutoCAD before you commit to the lengthy rendering process. To preview frames 1, pick the **Preview a scene** from the Animation menu, as follows:

```
Command: <pick Preview a scene>
Name of script to preview <C:\ACAD\ATK>: <Enter>
Frame number (press RETURN to view a range): 1
Searching script ><
```

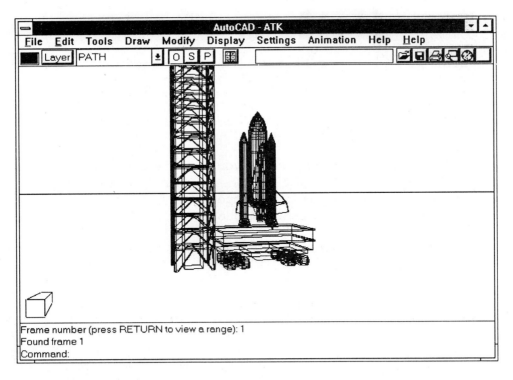

The Preview command displays the view along the camera path at camera position 1. The Dview command is used by ATK to show a perspective view that exactly duplicates a wireframe version of the rendered view created later (see Figure). The line that crosses the screen is the ellipse path polyline.

TIP NUMBER 33

Viewing a Series

The **Animation | Preview a Scene** command lets you watch a series of views—a very slow means of animation—right inside of AutoCAD! The **Preview** command does not display views past the last frame. You cannot, for example, go from frame 45 to frame 5; Preview stops at frame 50. ∎

Tutorial 3
AutoCAD-Rendered Animations

If you don't want to use AutoShade, you can still create shaded animations with AutoCAD. The ATK code will use AutoCAD's Shade command; Autodesk has not updated the code to use AutoCAD's Render command.

1. Pick **.SLD walkthrough** from the Animation pop-down menu, as follows:

   ```
   Command: <pick .SLD walkthrough>
   sldview PATH script to use <\Temp\ATK>: <Enter>
   Apply hide? <N>: <Enter>
   Apply AutoCAD Shading <N>: <Enter>
   ```

2. The Sldview command gives the choice of removing the hidden lines from each wireframe view (a painfully slow process) or to apply AutoCAD's own Shade command (significantly faster) to each view. The type of shading applied depends on the setting of the Shadedge system variable:

ShadEdge System Variable Values

ShadEdge	Style of shading
0	256-color flat shading
1	256-color outlined shading
2	Hidden-line removal
3	16-color flat shading

3. Remember to save the ATK drawing before ending the drawing session. When you finish setting up the camera path in AutoCAD, the Animation Tool Kit creates four files: Atk.Scr, Atk.Flm, Atk.Mvi, and 00Atk00.

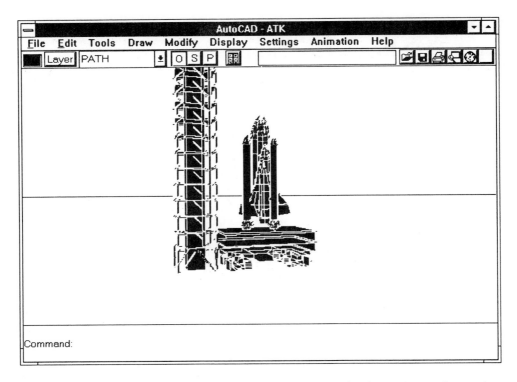

AutoShade and Flimaker uses these files to compile the animated movie:

- **Atk.Flm** is a filmroll file, which describes the AutoCAD drawing to AutoShade.

- **Atk.Scr** is an script file for AutoShade containing the instructions to automatically render the 50 frames we created in AutoCAD.

- **Atk.Mvi** is a Flimaker script file, which contains instructions for Flimaker to automatically compile the 50 rendered frames into a single FLI movie file.

- **00Atk00** is a dummy file created by the Animation Tool Kit to reassure itself that the subdirectory exists. You may erase it.

4. AutoShade uses the Atk.Scr script file to recreate the camera positions defined in AutoCAD with the Animation Tool Kit. Atk.Scr instructs AutoShade to render each frame to disk as RND rendering files, named Atk0001.Rnd through Atk0050.Rnd. Before running the Atk.Scr file via AutoShade, you need to reconfigure AutoShade for animations.

Configuring AutoShade

For Flimaker to accept the rendered output from AutoShade, you must reconfigure AutoShade to meet Flimaker's requirements. So throw out that $3,000 special-purpose 24-bit graphics board and install a $59 basic VGA—because that's all you'll need.

1. Start AutoShade with the reconfigure switch, as follows:

   ```
   C:\shade2\> shade /r
   ```

2. As AutoShade prompts you, type in the numbers that match your computer's pointing device (probably "#3, Microsoft mouse") and display device (probably "#5, VGA").

3. When you get to rendering display device, select option 7, "IBM Video Graphics Array (VGA 256 colors)."

4. Continue selecting the other hardware options to suit your needs. You probably say "Yes" to the questions asking about sharing a single screen and "None" for the rendering hardcopy device.

Tutorial 4
Rendering the Filmroll

With AutoShade configured for creating animations with Flimaker, you have it run the script file to generate the rendered frames for the animation.

1. Start the ATK.Scr script file by selecting the **File | Start Script** command.

2. When the **Select Script File** dialog box appears, select ATK then click on **OK**.

3. Sit back and wait as AutoShade renders each of the 50 frames, one by one (see Figure).

The time to finish the rendering varies according to the complexity and quality of the renderings, and the speed of your computer.
Using the Fastshade option on my 40 Mhz 386 takes about 10 minutes.
    A slower computer, or using the fullshade and intersection-checking options, takes longer.

4. When AutoShade is finished creating the rendering, exit the program by selecting **File | Quit**.

5. Look in the subdirectory: you find 50 RND files, named Atk0001.Rnd to Atk0050.Rnd, taking up about three megabytes of disk space. These files are compiled by the Flimaker program into the movie file.

Tutorial 5
Compile the Animation

Once shaded by AutoShade, the 50 rendering files are compiled together into a single movie file using the Flimaker program. This operation should also be done outside of Windows.

1. While still in DOS, instruct Flimaker to compile the movie with the following command:

   ```
   C:\shade2\> flimaker -v atk.mvi atk
   ```

   The -v (short for view) switch lets you watch as each frame is compiled. Leave out the switch to compile the movie twice as fast.

   The file Atk.Mvi contains the list of names of rendered files that Flimaker should use. You may encounter a bug here. The file may incorrectly list files with the SLD file extension, as follows:

   ```
   ATK0001.SLD
   ATK0002.SLD
   . . .
   ATK0050.SLD
   ```

   If it does, load the file into a text editor and use its search-and-replace command to change all occurrences of SLD to RND. When done, the Atk.Sld file should look like this:

   ```
   ATK0001.rnd
   ATK0002.rnd
   . . .
   ATK0050.rnd
   ```

   At the end of the Flimaker command line, the "Atk" is the name of the movie file. Flimaker automatically adds on the FLI extension.

2. After about two minutes of processing, the movie is compiled and is ready for viewing. I find it interesting that the 3 MB of rendering files have been compressed into a single 220 KB movie file, Atk.Fli.

Tutorial 6
Kinetic Animation

A kinetic animation moves objects instead of the camera. This kind of animation is handled differently from a path animation. The path animation creates a single filmroll file; a kinetic animation creates one filmroll file for every change in position of the objects. The reason is that a path filmroll file changes the camera position by simply defining new camera and target coordinates. Each frame in a kinetic animation repositions parts of the drawing. The camera remains static or it moves.

In this tutorial, you place the camera at a fixed point to watch the shuttle lift off its launch pad, as follows:

1. Load AutoCAD for Windows and the ATK drawing.

2. Make a new layer called LAUNCH; freeze the PATH and PATH_NUMBERS layers:

   Command: **layer m launch f path f path_numbers**

3. To select portions of the shuttle and to specify the flight path—all at the same time—split the screen in half. This lets you display two different views of the shuttle at the same time, as follows:

   Command: **vports 2 v**

4. In the left-hand viewport, make sure the viewpoint is the plan view and zoom out:

   Command: **vpoint 0,1,0**
   Command: **zoom .5x**
   Command: **usc v**

5. In the right-hand viewport, change the viewpoint to 1,1,-1 and zoom to the extents:

   Command: **vpoint 1,1,1**
   Command: **zoom e**

The view is from underneath looking up (see Figure).

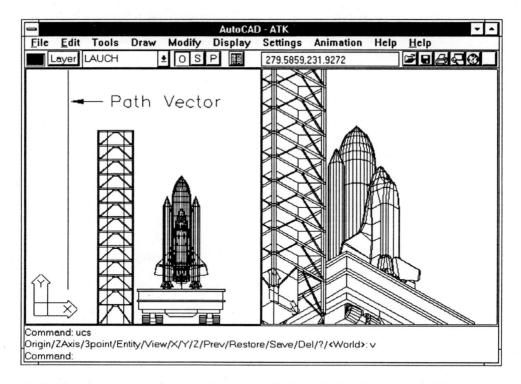

6. In the first tutorial, you drew a polyline circle (the round ellipse) for the camera path. For a kinetic animation, you draw a polyline called the "path vector." The polyline describes the length and the direction of the objects' movements. For the shuttle taking off from its launch pad, you draw a simple straight line with the 3dpoly command, as follows:

```
Command: 3dpoly
From point: 0,0,0
Close/Undo/<Endpoint of line>: 0,0,500
Close/Undo/<Endpoint of line>: <Enter>
```

While it doesn't matter where the polyline is located, the direction does matter. For the shuttle to launch into the air, draw the line in the up direction; otherwise, the shuttle will drive itself into the ground!

7. From the **Animation** menu item, select **ATK Setup** to create a new setup block. Use the name "LAU" (short for launch) for the name of the setup, and the filmroll name. Set the directory to place files as \Temp. Change the AutoShade output to Fastshade, unless you're prepared to wait for the longer Fullshade processing.

8. From the **Animation** menu item, select **Make a Camera Script** to create a new camera script, as follows:

```
Command: <select Make a Camera Script>
path ATK Setup to use: <pick ATK block>
Animation name <\Temp\>: \Temp\Lau<Enter>
Kinetic animation? <N> y
```

9. Specify a smaller number of frames than before (remember, each frame becomes a separate filmroll file):

```
Kinetic>> Number of filmrolls to use: 20
Kinetic>> Starting number <0001>: <Enter>
```

10. To create the launch effect, don't select the palindromic option (which would make the animation go back and forth):

```
Kinetic>> Sequential or Palindromic <S>: <Enter>
Kinetic>> Filmroll title <\Temp\>: lau
Number of Frames <20>: <Enter>
```

11. The position of the camera is fixed. Make your picks in the left-hand viewport:

```
Camera position: Path/Fixed/List <Path>: f
Camera, fixed view>> Pick a point (press RETURN to
   use a Scene): <Enter>
Camera scene: launch
```

12. Likewise, the *target* (the point that the camera is focussed on) is fixed on the center of the shuttle:

```
Target position: Fixed/Path/List <Fixed> f
Fixed target>> Pick a point: <pick center of
   shuttle>
```

13. The ATK LISP routine creates the script and movie files:

```
AutoShade script C:\shade2\lau.scr has been Created.
Animation list C:\shade2\lau.mvi has been Created.
```

14. With the role of the camera defined, you need to define the movement of the shuttle. From the **Animation** menu item, select **Animate Entities**, as follows:

```
Command: <pick Animate Entities>
Kinetic Please select ATK Setup to edit:
  <pick block>
Filmroll title <\Temp\>: lau
Number of frames: 20
Starting number <0001>: <Enter>
```

15. Now you go on to select the entities you want to animate. Select the shuttle and three rockets in the left-hand viewport (see Figure above):

```
[Entity Selection]
*press RETURN when finished*
Select objects: c
First corner: <pick>
Other corner: <pick>
4 found Select objects: <Enter>
```

16. With the entities selected, you go on to define the range and nature of the animation:

```
[Motion Range]
Start motion at frame <1>: <Enter>
Stop motion at frame <20>: <Enter>
```

17. The motion starts at frame #1 and ends with frame #20. The motion is fixed about a point (called a "node" here). Go back to making your screen picks in the left-hand viewport:

```
Entity motion: Path/Fixed/List <Path>: p
Motion path>> select a polyline: <pick 3dpoly line>
Reverse path <N>: <Enter>
```

18. The LISP routine loops back to let you define the motion of other objects. You decline the offer for now:

```
[Entity Selection]
*press RETURN when finished*
Select objects: <Enter>
Are you finished with the selection process? <Y>: y
```

19. You want the frames output to an FLM filmroll file for processing by AutoShade. The LISP routines creates 20 filmroll files, one for each frame in the animation. The process takes about 15 minutes:

```
Current output is to filmroll
Set output format to Drawing/Filmroll/Slide/Test
<filmroll>: <Enter>
Output format is set to filmroll
Making C:\shade2\lau0001.flm
...
Making C:\shade2\lau0020.flm
```

20. As the LISP routine does its work, you see the shuttle move through
     its 20 positions (see Figure). When the process is finished, don't save
     the drawing, exit AutoCAD, and exit Windows.

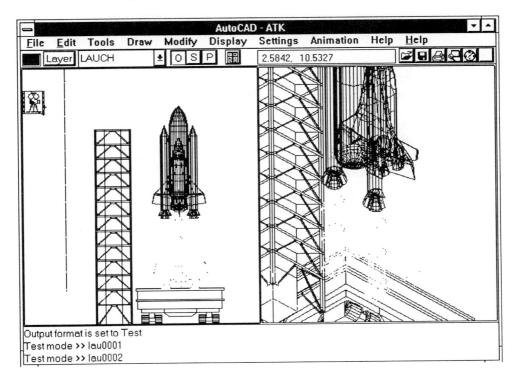

21. Start AutoShade and load the Lau.Scr file. Wait for Shade to process
     the 20 filmroll files, which takes about 20 minutes. Exit AutoShade.
         When you look in the \Shade2 subdirectory, you see 20 FLM files
     taking up about 1.6 MB. Erase the files to free up the disk space.

22. Run Flimaker to compile the 20 RND rendered files into a FLI movie file:

```
C:\shade2\> flimaker -v lau.mvi lau
```

Once Flimaker is done, go into Windows to view the animation with the Animation Player or the Media Player.

Summary

In this chapter, you learned how to create several kinds of animation with a 3D AutoCAD drawing. In the next chapter, you learn to run the animation with the Autodesk Animation Player or the Windows Media Player.

Motion and Sound

L ast chapter you saw how to animate AutoCAD drawings. The second part to animation is playback. In this chapter, you find out how to play the animation within Windows. The chapter also describes two software packages that edit WAV sound files created in Chapter 9.

Executive Summary

Watch your animations with the Autodesk's AaPlay application, which comes in several flavors:

- AaPlay runs under DOS or in the DOS box of Windows

- AaWin is a Windows application that runs under Windows v3.x

- A driver for the Windows Media Player that lets the application display Autodesk animations

Listen and edit your audio notes with free and shareware applications:

- Digital Audio Transport, by Voyetra, is included free with the ATI Stereo F/X board.

- Sound Editor, by Keith Boone, is shareware with a large number of editing functions

Tutorial 1
View the Animation with AaPlay

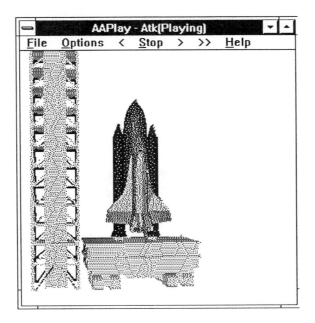

Last chapter you compiled the frames into an animation. Make sure you have the Animation Player for Windows, called "AaPlay" for short, installed on your computer. The software is on the disks supplied with the Animator Pro Bonus Pack labelled "Autodesk Animation Player for Windows." It is also available on the bonus diskette available with this book.

Animation
Player

1. To view the animation, load the Animation Player for Windows program by double-clicking on the hummingbird icon.

2. From the AaWin menu bar, select **File**, then pick **Open Animation**.

3. In the subdirectory, double-click on the filename, Atk.Fli. AaWin loads the Atk animation and displays the first frame (see Figure).

4. Pick the double-angle bracket >> play symbol. The view rotates around the shuttle at a speed of about 15 frames per second. The actual speed depends on the speed of your computer and its graphics board.

The control buttons are reversed from what you may be used to from VCRs and cassette players:

>> Click on the play button to start the animation; this is *not* the fast-forward button.

Stop Click on Stop to stop the animation.

< This button backspaces the animation, one frame at a time.

> This button moves the animation forward by one frame; this is *not* the play button.

Tutorial 2
View the Animation with Media Player

As an alternative to AaPlay, you can use the Media Player supplied by Windows v3.1 and Windows for Workgroups. As the previous chapter introduced, Media Player plays WAV sound files and MIDI music files. When you install AaPlay, it adds a driver so that the Media Player can also play Autodesk Animator animation files with FLC, FLI, and AAS extensions.

1. Double-click on the Media Player icon, then select **File** from the menu bar and pick **Open**.

2. When the dialog box opens up, click on the down arrow next to **List Files of Type...** and select "Animation1" (see Figure)

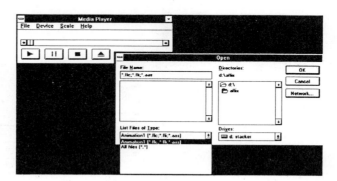

3. Load the Atk.Fli animation file. Click on the play button (▸) and Media Player runs through the animation once. There is no automatic repeat, as with Autodesk's Player.

Change the Playback Speed

There are two ways to change the playback speed of the animation to run faster or slower.

Change Speed with AaWin. The easier method is to change the speed from within AaWin. Pick **File** from the menu bar, and then select **Anim Settings...** (see Figure). The **Animation Settings** dialog box displays the animation's current settings in the upper-right corner. The dialog box lets you set a number of speed-related parameters, as follows:

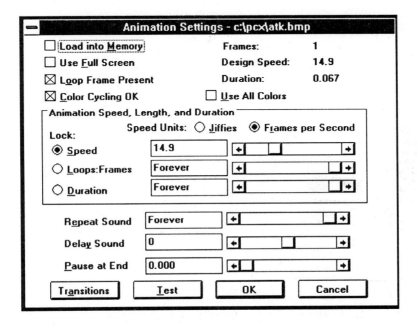

- ▸ **Load into Memory.** Loading the animation into memory makes it run smoother.

- ▸ **Use Full Screen.** Running the animation full screen makes it run smoother. However, animations compiled at 320 x 200 occupy only a part of the full-size screen.

- ▸ **Speed Units.** If *Jiffies*, a smaller number is faster; 0 is fastest. If *Frames per Second*, a larger number is faster; 51 fps is fastest.

- ▸ **Speed.** Move the slider with your mouse, or type in a value in the enter box.

TIP NUMBER 35
What are Jiffies?

Jiffies is a good term for programmers but not that useful for producers, who deal in fps (frames per second). AaWin performs a jiffies-to-fps conversion, which may not apply to your system.

You may want to calibrate your computer hardware in fps. Be aware that the duration of a jiffy increases with more complex animations. On my computer, I calibrated the shuttle animation by timing with a stop watch ten rotations of the shuttle (500 frames) and got the following results, which match fairly closely the Animation Player's estimates:

Jiffies Calibration

Jiffies	My FPS	AaWin FPS
1	51.0	39.0
2	34.5	34.1
3	23.3	23.1
4	17.5	17.3
5	14.1	14.1

■

Picking the **Test** button lets you see the effect of the changed parameters, returning you to the **Animation Settings** dialog box. When you're satisfied with the result, pick **OK**.

Change Speed with FliMaker. The Media Player doesn't let you adjust the animation speed, so you'll need to go back to DOS. Recompile the movie with FliMaker and add a digit to the command line, as follows:

```
C:\shade2\> flimaker -v atk.mvi atk 2
```

The "2" specifies the delay time between frames as two jiffies, effectively speeding up the animation (the default value is five jiffies). At zero jiffies, the movie runs as fast as the computer hardware allows.

Modifying the ATK Files

Once you have the animation roughed to your satisfaction, you go back to AutoShade and improve the quality. You'll get more accurate animation by changing the Fastshade option to Fullshade.

You cannot take advantage of AutoShade's Quickshade and Smoothshade options. If you do, Flimaker complains, "Item in file is not a colour mapped polygon" and won't compile the rendered frames.

You don't need to go back into AutoCAD to make the changes; instead you edit the Atk.Scr file. Here is the header and first frame of Atk.Scr script file:

```
.*******************************************************
. *   ATK.SCR
. * Path - Camera path animation script for AutoShade.
. * Total frames: 50
. * Source drawing: ATK.DWG
.*******************************************************
record on
open atk
spercent -1
perspective on
lens 30
  . *
. **FRAME 1***********************
  . *
target 7.0000,13.0000,0.0000
camera 7.0000,-95.8396,0.0000
fastshade ATK0001
  . *
```

Lines beginning with a period are comment lines, which are ignored by AutoShade.

To change from Fastshade to Fullshade, use the search-and-replace function to change all occurrences of "fastshade" to "fullshade."

Try changing "lens 30" to "lens 50" or "lens 70" to move the shuttle closer. You can also monkey around with the Spercent and Perspective values. After making the changes, the file looks like this:

```
record on
open atk
spercent -1
perspective on
lens 70
```

```
.  *
.  **FRAME 1************************
.  *
target 7.0000,13.0000,0.0000
camera 7.0000,-95.8396,0.0000
fullshade ATK0001
.  *
```

To see the effect of the changes, save the file, and rerun AutoShade and Flimaker, as follows:

```
C:\shade2\> shade /satk
C:\shade2\> flimaker -v atk.mvi atk2
C:\shade2\> win aawin
```

Now you can view the animation with the AaWin animation player.

Sound Editor
Digital Audio Transport

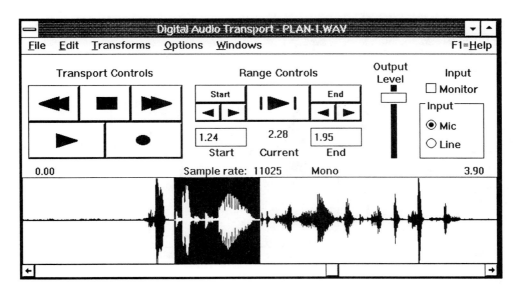

ATI
3761 Victoria Park Avenue
Scarborough, ON M1W 3S2
(416) 756-0718

ATI bundles in Voyetra's WinDAT (short for Windows digital audio transport) program with the Stereo F/X sound board. WinDAT lets you edit WAV sound files, including those produced by Autodesk's Anotes program.

In the figure below, I've loaded one of the sound files I created in Chapter 9 ("Audio Notes"). Remember, you need to change the extension of the stored sound file from "Axx" to "Wav."

The waveform shown in the figure is the digital representation of me saying, "Check with client on the arrangement of the kitchen." I've blocked two words, "...with client...", shown in reverse video. The Range Controls let me adjust the blocked range. After you select a range, you can delete it (creating the sentence "Check ... on the arrangement of the kitchen") or modify the sound characteristics.

Or, you can move (cut 'n paste) words around, add in other sounds. After the sound has been edited, you can save it. Renaming the extension back to Axx lets AutoCAD vocalize the changed audio note.

Wave Editor

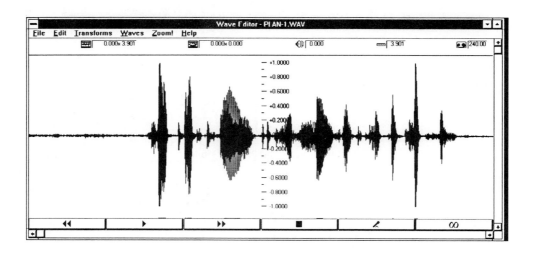

Keith W. Boone
114 Broward Street
Tallahassee, FL 32301

 Wave Editor ($20; shareware) is a Windows program that modifies and analyzes waveforms. It is limited to working with 8-bit monophonic WAV files. You load and playback the WAV file. Clicking on the button with the infinity symbol plays the WAV file over and over. The vertical slider (on the left) increases and decreases the scale of the waveform, letting you make very accurate edits.

Like the Sound Recorder included with Windows, Wave Editor lets you reverse, change the volume, and add echo to the file. Unlike Sound Recorder, Wave Editor has many more special effects. It performs polar and rectangular FFT (fast fourier transforms). You can apply low-pass, high-pass, band-pass, and band-reject filters.

You can create your own sound files from mathematically pure waveforms, such as cosine, triangle, square, sawtooth, and just plain noise. The Cut, Copy, Paste, and Duplicate commands let you change the sound clip—for example, creating a stuttering effect.

Programming
AutoCAD

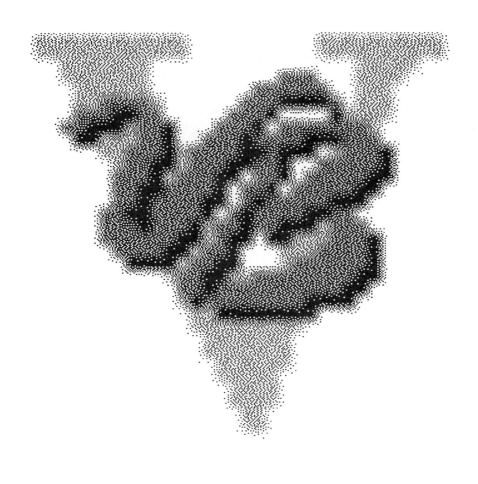

The Toolbar
and Toolbox

T o Autodesk's credit, AutoCAD for Windows improves the ways you customize AutoCAD. Most significant are the Toolbar and Toolbox, which let you assign macros (frequently-used commands) to a button on-the-fly. Programming the Toolbar and Toolbox is as easy as clicking the mouse's right button and typing in a command name. This chapter gives you a tour of the Toolbar and Toolbox, which operate very similarly. It includes tutorials on how to program with macros.

Executive Summary

The Windows version of AutoCAD provides two user interface enhancements not found in the DOS version: the Toolbar and the Toolbox.

The Toolbar:
- ▸ Replaces the status line of the DOS version of AutoCAD
- ▸ Gives fast access to the Entity Creation Modes dialogue box, the Layer Control dialogue box, a list box of non-frozen layer names, the Toolbox, coordinate display mode, and programmable icon buttons
- ▸ Program an icon by clicking on the button with the mouse's right button

The Toolbox:
- ▸ Sticks to the left or right edges of the drawing screen; or floats anywhere on the desktop
- ▸ Gives fast access to frequently used commands, AutoLISP routines and ADS applications
- ▸ Program an icon by clicking on the button with the mouse's right button

Looking at the Toolbar

In Windows, the Toolbar replaces the AutoCAD status line of the DOS version. The Toolbar displays all the information of the old status line, plus offers significant new features (see Figure).

From left to right, the functions of the Toolbar are:

- The current working color
- The Layer button
- The first characters of the current layer name
- The status of snap, ortho, and paper space modes
- The x,y-coordinates
- Programmable buttons

Let's look at how each of these functions work.

Color Box. By clicking on the color box, you bring up the **Entity Creation Modes** dialogue box (see Figure) In macros, the dialogue box is displayed by the 'Ddemodes command. The dialogue box has buttons that bring up further dialogue boxes to change the color, layers, linetypes, and text styles, as well as the set the elevation and thickness.

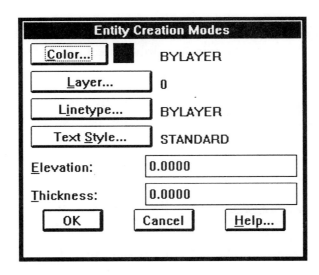

Layer Button. The Layer button was added in Release 12 for Windows. It brings up the **Layer Control** dialogue box (see Figure). In macros, the dialogue box is displayed by the DdLmodes command. The dialogue box lets you control all aspects of layers, including setting their color, linetype, and visibility.

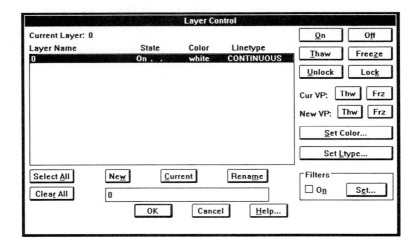

Layer Name. The Toolbar is no longer limited to displaying just the first eight characters of the current layer name. The default font displays about 14 characters, while selecting a smaller font with the **Preferences** command increases the number of displayable characters (AutoCAD layer names can be up to 31 characters in length).

Layer List Box. New in Release 12 for Windows is the list box that displays all layers in the drawing in alphabetical order. Here's how to use the list box:

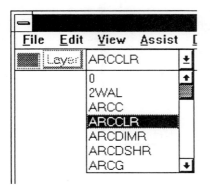

1. Click on the down arrow next to the layer name. The list box displays seven layer names at a time.

2. The scroll arrows let you view the other layer names. Click the down arrow on the scroll bar to see other layer names.

3. To make current another layer, click on its name. AutoCAD uses the Layer command to set the layer.

Preprogrammed Buttons. The Toolbar buttons labelled O, S, and P are preprogrammed to toggle the state of ortho, snap, and paper space modes. When you click on a button to turn a mode on, the button changes its look—as if it is depressed. You cannot change the meaning of these three buttons.

Programmable Buttons. There are two clusters of programmable buttons, grouped on either side of the coordinate display. The number of buttons available on the Toolbar depends on the resolution that AutoCAD is running at, as shown in the following table:

Toolbar Buttons Available

AutoCAD	Resolution	Tbarxx.Dll	Left Group	Right Group	Total Buttons
VGA	640 x 480	Tbar16.Dll	2	6	8
Super VGA	800 x 600	Tbar16.Dll	6	10	16
Extended VGA	1024 x 768	Tbar24.Dll	4	15	19
...	1280 x 1024	Tbar32.Dll	5	19	24
...	1600 x 1200	Tbar32.Dll	6	20	26

The number of programmable buttons depends on which Tbar DLL (dynamic link library) is used. The Tbar file defines the look and size of the icons. AutoCAD Release 11 for Windows comes with three Tbar files: Tbar16.Dll, Tbar24.Dll, and Tbar32.Dll. Release 12 dropped Tbar32.Dll.

The number in the Tbar filename refers to the bitmap size of the icons. The "16" means the icons are 16 x 16 pixels in size. The small size is suitable for low resolution displays, such as 640 x 480, and for displaying more buttons on high-resolution displays.

Six Toolbar buttons are defined by Autodesk for commonly-used commands:

Toggle display and position of Toolbox

Open a drawing file

Save the drawing file

Print the drawing

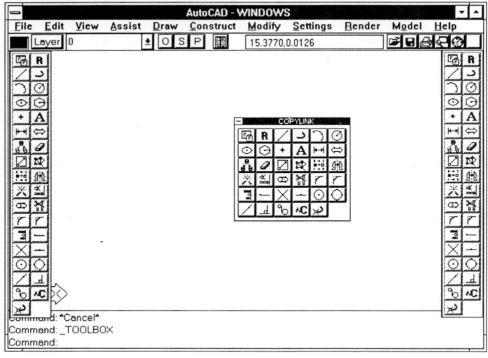

Start the Zoom command

Toggle display of the Aerial View (see chapter 3).

Coordinate Display. The coordinate display reads out the current x,y-coordinates. By pressing **<F6>**, **<Ctrl>-D**, or clicking on the coordinate display, you toggle between static, dynamic, and relative displays, as follows:

- ▸ **Static** updates the coordinate display only when you click the mouse.
- ▸ **Dynamic** updates the coordinate display whenever the mouse moves.
- ▸ **Relative** displays the distance and angle from the last mouse click.

Looking at the Toolbox

New to Release 12 for Windows is the Toolbox, a group of icons that execute commands and macros. You access the Toolbox by clicking on the Toolbox button (next to the "P" paper space button). Four clicks makes the Toolbox appear in three locations (see Figure):

- **Locked to the left edge** of the AutoCAD drawing screen; replaces the side-screen menu. Toolbox icons cannot branch to sub-toolbox.

- **Floating on the Windows desktop.** The Toolbox is repositionable anywhere on the desktop; not limited to the AutoCAD window. Icon name is displayed on the title bar when cursor passes over.

- **Locked to the right edge** of the AutoCAD drawing screen.

Clicking a fourth time makes the Toolbox disappear. When the Toolbox is locked in position, it does not display an icon label—an inconvenience.

Change the Shape of the Toolbox. You can change the width of the Toolbox by clicking on any Toolbox icon with the mouse's right button. The **Toolbox Customization** dialogue box appears (see Figure):

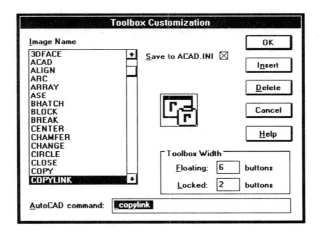

In the lower right corner is the **Toolbox Width** area with two text entry boxes. The default values are:
- **Floating:** 6 buttons
- **Locked:** 2 buttons

Since the Toolbox always consists of 36 buttons, setting the width automatically sets the height. When you make a change to the two values, the values are stored in the Acad.Ini file, unless you turn off **Save to Acad.Ini** by clicking on the check box.

Default Configuration. Autodesk configured the Toolbox with 36 icons that execute the following commands:

🔲	_copylink
R	_redraw
╱	_line
⤵	_pline
◗	_arc
◷	_circle
◉	_ellipse
⬡	_polygon
✦	_point
A	_dtext
↔	_ddim
⇔	_move
🔁	_copy
✐	_erase
◰	_scale
✗	_rotate
⠿	_change
⚱	_mirror
✸	_break
⬓	_extend
⊕	_stretch
✂	_trim
⌐	_fillet
⌐	_chamfer
◲	_align
—	_endp
✕	_int
—	_mid
⊙	_center
◇	_quad
╱	_near
⊥	_per
⦿	_tan
↻	*Cancel*
↲	_pedit
↲	

Creating Macros on the Fly

The purpose of the Toolbar and Toolbox buttons is to let you create macros on the fly, which you access with a simple click on the associated icon.

A *macro* collects several commands into a single icon pick. The macro is anything from a single command that you use often (such as "Save") to a series of commands that make drawing and editing easier, such as "Erase L".

Tutorial 1
Program a Single Command

The easiest macro to program is a single command. Here's how to assign the U (undo the most recent command) command to a Toolbar button (programming a Toolbox button follows the same procedure):

1. To program a button, move the cursor over any button on the Toolbar. For this tutorial, choose the blank button (button 7) next to the Aerial View button.

2. Click the mouse's rightmost button. This action brings up the **AutoCAD Toolbar Button** dialogue box (see Figure).

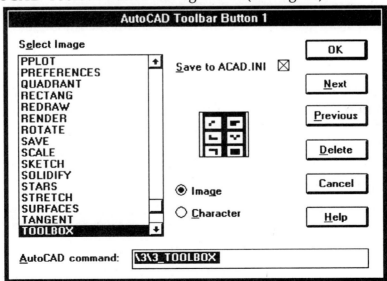

You can redefine any Toolbar button except the first three, which are labelled O, S, and P; any Toolbox button can be redefined. You can assign a macro to an empty button (one that has no label on it) or change the meaning of a labeled button.

3. In the edit box, type in the command name, U. Make sure you type a space after the U to act as the **<Enter>** key. If there is another macro in the box, erase the old text by highlighting the text and pressing the **<Delete>** key.

4. You have the choice of labelling the button in two ways:

   ▸ Click on the **Character** radio button to select a character A to Z.

   ▸ Click on the **Image** radio button to select one of the 84 predefined icons; you cannot easily create custom icons.

   In this case, click on the **Character** radio button and select the letter **U** from the list box.

5. If an X appears next to **Save to Acad.Ini**, the new button definition is saved for future AutoCAD sessions; if you don't want the definition saved when you exit AutoCAD, click on the check box.

6. Pick the **OK** button to exit the dialogue box; if you goofed up, pick **Cancel** instead to ignore the changes and exit the dialogue box. After the dialogue box disappears, the newly defined Toolbar button should be labelled with a U.

7. Try out the button by clicking on the U button on the Toolbar. The screen blinks as the last command is undone. (Toolbar definitions are not affected by the U and Undo commands.)

Other single-command macros that might be useful are: Blipmode, Color, Ddedit, Dim, Dim1, Files, Fill, Grid, Hide, Id, Isoplane, Oops, Plan, Qtext, Redraw, Redrawall, Regen, Regenall, Shade, and Textscr. The Graphscr command does not work since the button isn't accessible when you need to use it.

Tutorial 2
Commands with an Option

Now that you've assigned a single command to a Toolbar button, here's how to assign a command with an option to a Toolbar button.

Autodesk's *Using AutoCAD for Windows* manual states that the Zoom icon (button 5) executes the Zoom Windows command; it doesn't. By reprogramming the button with Zoom W, AutoCAD automatically executes the Zoom command and chooses the Window option. In using the Zoom Window command, you normally type at the Command: prompt the following:

```
Command: zoom <spacebar>
All/Center/Dynamic/Extents/Left/Previous/
Vmax/Window/<Scale(X/XP)>: w <spacebar>
First corner:
```

To write a macro, you mimic what you type at the Command prompt:

```
zoom<space>
w<space>
```

Let's try it:

1. Click the mouse's right button on the Toolbar's Zoom button and the **AutoCAD Toolbox Button** dialogue box appears.

2. In the edit box, click the mouse's left button at the end of the existing _ZOOM text. Add the "W" and space just as if you were typing the commands at the Command: prompt, as follows:

```
_ZOOM w<spacebar>
```

TIP NUMBER 36
Other Toolbar Characters

If you're in a hurry, you don't need to assign a character or bitmap to the button. Click on the **Character** radio button but don't click on a letter of the alphabet. AutoCAD automatically assigns the first character of the macro to the button.

This is also a workaround for assigning a character that isn't an alphabetical character: lowercase characters, numbers, and punctuation. ∎

Make sure you press the spacebar after the W, otherwise the command won't continue on its own.

3. The Zoom Window command can be used during other commands by making the command transparent. Click at the beginning of the macro and add an apostrophe, as follows (see Figure):

'_ZOOM w

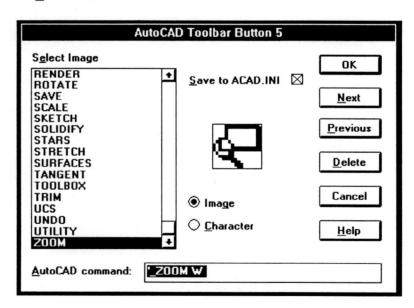

4. Save the macro by clicking on the **OK** button.

5. After the dialogue box disappears, try out the redefined button by clicking on the Zoom icon. AutoCAD starts the Zoom command,

supplies the Window option, and prompts you to pick the first corner of the windows, as follows:

```
Command: zoom
All/Center/Dynamic/Extents/Left/Previous/Vmax/
   Window/<Scale(X/XP)>: w
First corner: <pick>
Other corner: <pick>
```

Other single-option macros that might be useful are: Erase L, Expert 5, Fillet R, List L, Pdmode 1, Pdsize 1, Quit C, Select C, Shadedge 2, Undo M, Vports J, Zoom 0.85x, and Zoom V.

Tip Number 38
Cancel Previous Command

If a command shouldn't be transparent, prefix it with the sequence **\3\3\3** to cancel a pending command. The \3 is shorthand for Cancel or <Ctrl>-C; three \3 ensure that any command is canceled, even if AutoCAD is deep down in the Pedit command.

To apply the triple-cancel sequence to the above macro, erase the apostrophe, and add the three \3's. The macro should now look as follows:

\3\3\3_ZOOM w

Tutorial 3
A Complex Macro

You've seen how to assign a simple macro to a Toolbar button. Try assigning a more complex macro to the Toolbox. In this tutorial, you use AutoLISP (AutoCAD's programming language) load the sample LISP routine Project.Lsp. At the Command: prompt, you would type the following:

```
Command: (load "\\acadwin\\sample\\project")<Enter>
```

Once again, mimic what you type at the Command: prompt by writing the macro, as follows:

1. If the Toolbox is not on the screen, click the Toolbox icon (button 1, next to the "P") to make it appear.

2. Click on any icon with the mouse's right button to make the **Toolbox Customization** dialogue box appear.

3. Click on the **AutoCAD command:** text box and any existing macro is highlighted. As you begin to type the new macro, the existing macro disappears. Type as if you were typing the commands at the Command: prompt, as follows:

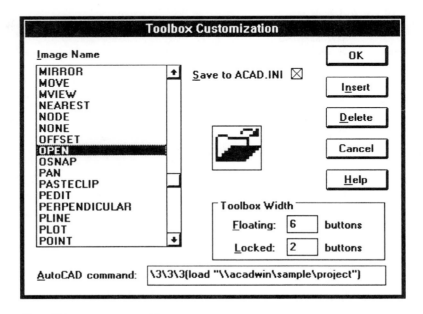

```
\3\3\3(load "\\acad\\sample\\project")
```

Make sure you press the spacebar after the final ")". Recall that the three "\3" cancel any command in progress and that the double backslashes "\\" represent a single backslash to DOS.

4. Since AutoCAD has no icon for this macro, pick any icon that appeals to you and makes sense as a LISP loader: the icon associated with the **Open** command might be a good choice (see Figure). Unlike the Toolbar, the Toolbox does not support use of single characters.

5. When you click the **OK** button, AutoCAD save the button assignment (to the Acad.Ini file) and exits the dialogue box.

6. Try out the new button for loading the LISP routine. Click on the file folder icon; the Project.Lsp routine loads.

Other complex macros that might be useful to you include:

- Setup up multiple viewports
- Switch between UCS planes
- Insert blocks
- Switch between elevations
- Rotate objects by the same angle
- Update externally referenced drawings
- Set a new working layer

Toolbar Yeas and Nays

You should be aware two limitations to Toolbar macros:

1. The maximum length of macro is 79 characters

2. You cannot use the metacharacters employed by menu macros. Most seriously, you cannot use the backslash to pause for user input. Instead, you use the following ASCII codes:

Toolbar and Toolbox Metacharacters

Metacharacter	Meaning
<Space>	<Enter>
;	Suppress space character
\n	Return
\t	Tab
****	\ (slash character)
\nnn	ASCII nnn
\2	Toggle snap mode
\3	Cancel
\4	Toggle coordinate display
\5	Toggle isoplane
\7	Toggle grid mode

Editing Toolbar and Toolbox with Acad.Ini

If you want to program all 26 Toolbar and 36 Toolbox buttons at once, it is faster to edit the Acad.Ini file (found in the \Acadwin subdirectory) with the Windows Notebook text editor (see Figure).

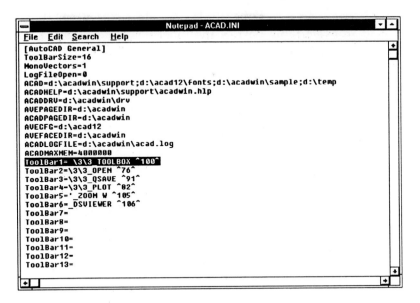

Halfway down the [AutoCAD General] section, you see a number of lines beginning with the word "ToolBar." The first seven ToolBar entries probably look like this (unless you've modified them already):

```
ToolBar1=\3\3_TOOLBOX ^100^
ToolBar2=\3\3_OPEN ^76^
ToolBar3=\3\3_QSAVE ^91^
ToolBar4=\3\3_PLOT ^82^
ToolBar5='_ZOOM W ^105^
ToolBar6=_DSVIEWER ^106^
ToolBar7=
```

Each entry consists of five parts, as follows:

▶ **ToolBar** refers to the Toolbar, rather than the ToolBox.

▶ ToolBar**1** (number one) refers to the first programmable button on the ToolBar.

▶ ToolBar1 **=** (equals sign) is the assignment character.

- `ToolBar1=\3\3_TOOLBOX` is the macro assigned to the first button on the ToolBar; this macro toggles the state of the ToolBox.

- `ToolBar1=\3\3_TOOLBOX ^100^` (carat, one hundred, caret) is the icon assigned to the first button of the ToolBar. Icon 100 is the ToolBox icon; the surrounding carat symbols (^) alert AutoCAD that the icon number is an executable part of the macro.

    (This is a change from AutoCAD Release 11 for Windows, which uses a name for the icon. For example, in Release 11 the erase icon is ^ERASE^.)

When you use a character in place of an icon, the entry in the Acad.Ini file looks like this:

```
ToolBar1=\3\3_TOOLBOX #T
```

The hash character (#) acts as the delimiter to alert AutoCAD that the character T is the symbol to display on the button.

Changing the Button Size

If you have a large monitor (such as 16" or 19") hooked up to a high-resolution graphics board, then you can afford to display smaller buttons. If you have difficulty reading the icons or picking the buttons with the mouse, you might prefer larger icons. If you'd like the size of the buttons to be larger or smaller than what AutoCAD picked, all it takes is a simple edit of the Acad.Ini file.

Using Windows Notebook text editor, load the Acad.Ini file. Look for the line that read `ToolBarSize=`, which you'll find under the section entitled `[AutoCAD General]`.

Change the number that's there to 16 (for smaller buttons), or 24 for medium-size buttons. (In Release 11 for Windows, you can supply the value 32 for even larger buttons.)

```
[AutoCAD General]
ToolBarSize=24
```

The number corresponds to the Tbarxx.Dll file AutoCAD selects; the change does not take effect until the next time you load AutoCAD.

The size of the buttons depends on the resolution of your graphics board and the size of the monitor (see Figures). At 800 x 600 resolution, AutoCAD displays eleven 24-pixel-size buttons and sixteen 16-pixel-size buttons.

The small 16 x 16-pixel bitmap icons displayed by Tbar16.Dll:

The medium-size 24 x 24-pixel bitmap icons displayed by Tbar24.Dll:

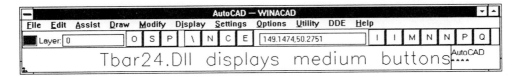

The large 32 x 32-pixel bitmap icons displayed by Tbar32.Dll (only available in Release 11 for Widows):

Summary

In this chapter, you learned how to program the Toolbar and Toolbox. In the next chapter, you find out how AutoCAD works with dynamic data exchange.

Dynamic Data Exchange

*T*he Clipboard makes it easy to transfer text and graphics between Windows applications. But the process is manual and transferring alphanumeric data by the Clipboard is difficult. Windows provides two automatic methods for programs to transfer data, text, and graphics: OLE was described in Chapter 6; DDE, short for dynamic data exchange, lets two or more Windows applications automatically exchange data. This chapter describes DDE and how to make it work with AutoCAD for Windows. It includes several tutorials to help you understand the operation of dynamic data exchange.

Executive Summary

In Windows, the DDE (dynamic data exchange) facility allows up to 16 applications to exchange data with each other as a background process. Some applications use DDE for their own purposes; for example, AutoCAD communicates with AutoLISP and ADS via DDE. Not all Windows applications are DDE-aware. More complicated than the Clipboard and OLE, DDE is meant for programmers.

There are two types of DDE links that can be set up:
- ▸ A hot link forces an exchange of data anytime the data changes
- ▸ A cold (or warm) link exchanges data only when instructed

For simple DDE work, AutoCAD for Windows includes the Dde.Lsp routine:
- ▸ First, load the Dde.Lsp routine: (load "dde")
- ▸ The Send command sends the entire drawing to an Excel worksheet
- ▸ The (sendset) function sends the current selection set
- ▸ The Get command retrieves all data from Excel

The ADS application, DdeLisp.Exe, contains AutoCAD's predefined DDE functions and must be loaded first with (xload "ddelisp").

There are five steps to setting up a DDE link with AutoCAD:
- ▸ Open a channel with the AppInit function
- ▸ Send data with one of five different functions: SendDrawing, EntPokeCell, PokeSet, PokeAll, PokeAllTbl, and PokeTblCell
- ▸ Execute commands remotely with the Execute function
- ▸ Request data with the ModDrawing function
- ▸ Close the channel with the Terminate function

AutoCAD sends data to the other DDE application in a DXF-like format.

History of DDE

IBM first introduced dynamic data exchange with its OS/2 operating system in 1987. In fact, the OS/2 version of AutoCAD Release 10 included the same DDE example—the parametric shaft—as in AutoCAD for Windows. Since then, Microsoft implemented DDE in its own Windows operating environment. IBM has gone on to create SOM (system object model), the OS/2 equivalent to OLE.

DDE has been implemented by Autodesk in Release 10 for OS/2, and Releases 11 and 12 for Windows. OLE was added to Release 12 and is not available in Release 11.

How DDE Works

Dynamic data exchange (DDE) allows two programs to exchange data in *realtime*. An immediate application is parametric design: one program controls the parameters of another program, with immediate feedback.

One example of parametric design is supplied with AutoCAD for Windows. A multipart shaft is drawn in three dimensions. Its design is controlled by an Excel worksheet (Excel's name for a spreadsheet file). When you change a value in the worksheet, the shaft drawing is updated in AutoCAD; similarly, when you stretch the length of the shaft, the values in the worksheet are updated.

The drawback to DDE is that it is not user friendly; it is meant for programmers and those who like to tinker with macros and operating systems. OLE, which is based on DDE, is user friendly but lacks the programming link.

DDE is a feature of Microsoft Windows, which the programmers of Windows applications elect to employ. The Autodesk implementation is oriented to exchanging DXF-like data with spreadsheets. AutoCAD's DDE facilities can be made to work with other applications—but only with awkward programming. For example, you can link programs written in Visual Basic with AutoCAD via DDE. In fact, AutoCAD and AutoLISP (and hence ADS) communicate with each other via a DDE link.

The Five Stages of DDE

There are five parts to the process of carrying out data communications via DDE:

Open a channel. By opening a *DDE channel* with another application, a link is created by Windows between the two applications. The channel is the link over which data is sent. Opening a channel may involve automatic launching of the other application.

In AutoCAD, use the **AppInit** function to launch the other application (if it isn't already running), open the data file (called the *topic*): this creates the DDE channel.

Send information. Once the DDE channel is established, AutoCAD sends its drawing data to the other application, such as the Excel worksheet. Windows is not limited to a single DDE channel. While AutoCAD is sending data to Excel, Excel in turn can be communicating with a third application, such as the Q+E database query program. AutoCAD sends data via DDE to the worksheet in six ways:

▸ Send the entire drawing to the worksheet with the new AutoLISP **SendDrawing** function

▸ Send a specific drawing entity to a specific cell address with the **EntPokeCell**

▸ Send a selection set with **PokeSet**

▸ Send all drawing entities the **PokeAll** function

▸ Send all table entries with the **PokeAllTbl** function

▸ Send selected table entries with the **PokeTblCell** function

Execute remote commands. In addition to sending data, AutoCAD can send commands to Excel. The commands instruct Excel to modify the data, perform calculations or apply lookup tables. Naturally, the instructions are Excel commands, not AutoCAD commands.

Use the **Execute** function to execute commands in the other application (called the "remote" application).

Request data. After the data is modified by Excel, AutoCAD can request the data be sent back to the drawing, which updates its drawing database.

Use the **ModDrawing** function to have AutoCAD update all or selected portions of its drawing database.

Close the channel. When you no longer need the DDE link, it is advisable to close the DDE channel. Closing the channel frees system resources, such as CPU and memory.

Use the **Terminate** command to shut down the DDE channel.

Hot and Warm Links

When it comes to creating the DDE link between two programs, you have two choices. You create a *hot link* or a *warm link*. Here are the differences:

▶ **Hot link.** When two programs are connected by a hot DDE link, a change in one program is automatically made—and with little delay—in the other program. The advantage is immediate feedback; the disadvantage is greater processing overhead and slightly slower operation all around.

▶ **Warm link.** When two programs are connected with a warm link, a change in one program is made only when you ask for an update (some Windows applications call this a "cold link"). The advantage is less processing overhead; the disadvantage is delayed response.

AutoCAD supports both temperatures of link. Sometimes a Regen or Zoom E command is required to see the result of an update—whether hot, warm, or cold.

Preparing for the Tutorials

The best way to understand dynamic data exchange is to try it out. AutoCAD's DDE-related functions are in an ADS application called "DdeLisp.Exe." You interface directly with DdeLisp using AutoLISP syntax or indirectly using AutoLISP routines.

Release 12 for Windows includes an AutoLISP program called "Dde.Lsp." The program demonstrates the DDE functions in DdeLisp.Exe with the Microsoft Excel worksheet. You may want to print out the Dde.Lsp file and read programmer Phil Ford's comments. In addition, the standard Acad.Mnu file for Windows includes DDE functions in menu form. You will find them under the **Edit** menu.

For these tutorials, I assume you know how to use Excel and are familiar with AutoLISP.

Tutorial 1
The Send and Get Commands

In this DDE tutorial, you create a simple AutoCAD drawing and send the drawing information to Excel. Once the data is in an Excel worksheet, you look it. Finally, you change the data and watch how the AutoCAD drawing change at the same time.

Dde.Lsp distills all the specialized DDE functions into one simple AutoLISP command: **Send**. Later, you use other AutoLISP functions to send and receive DDE data.

Try using Dde.Lsp as follows:

1. Load AutoCAD and open a new drawing called "ASDF." Load Dde.Lsp, as follows:

   ```
   Command: (load "dde")
   DDE.LSP and DDELISP.EXE loaded.
   ```

   Dde.Lsp automatically loads DdeLisp.Exe if the ADS application is not already loaded.

2. Draw three items (a white line, blue text, and a red circle on a couple of layers), as follows:

   ▸ A diagonal white line on layer 0

   ```
   Command: line
   From point: 1,1
   To point: 4,5
   To point: <Enter>
   ```

   ▸ Two lines of blue text on layer Notes

   ```
   Command: layer
   ?/Make/.../Thaw: make
   New layer name <0>: notes
   ?/Make/.../Thaw: color
   New layer color: blue
   Layer name(s) for color 5 (blue) <NOTES>: <Enter>
   ?/Make/.../Thaw: <Enter>

   Command: dtext
   Justify/Style/<Start point>: 3,2
   Height <0.2000>: 0.5
   ```

```
Rotation angle <0>: <Enter>
Text: Text at <Enter>
Text: (3,2) <Enter>
Text: <Enter>
```

▸ A 2" red circle on layer Notes

```
Command: color
New entity color (BYLAYER): red

Command: circle
3P/2P/<Center point>: end
of <pick upper end of line>
Diameter/<Radius>: 2
```

3. Size the drawing with the **Zoom E** command. When you are done, the drawing should look something like the Figure.

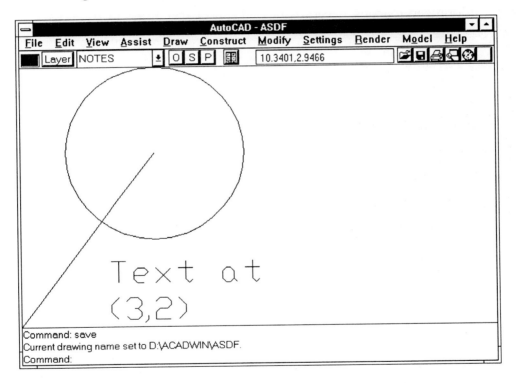

4. Save the drawing as "ASDF."

5. Send the ASDF drawing to Excel with the **Send** command, as follows:

```
Command: send
Sending drawing data...
Scanning drawing data...
Spreadsheet row:
Number of rows used by drawing: 78
```

Windows loads Excel and the default worksheet, called "Sheet1.Xls." AutoCAD sends the ASDF drawing data in a format similar to DXF (see Figure, next page). The Send command reports back that the drawing data used 78 rows in the worksheet. Later in this chapter we decode the meaning of the DXF format.

4. Display both programs—AutoCAD and Excel—on the screen at the same time by *tiling* the two windows. Make sure all applications are minimized to icons, except AutoCAD and Excel. Press **<Ctrl>-<Esc>** to

---

TIP NUMBER 39
The DDE Initialization File

The settings of the **DDE Initiate Conversation** dialogue box are stored in the DdeLisp.Ini file, found in the \Windows subdirectory. It consists of the following lines:

```
[AutoCAD DDE]
DDE App=Excel
DDE Topic=Sheet1
DDE Path=Excel.exe
DDE Advise=1
```

The INI information has the following meaning:

▸ The DDE App is the name of the DDE-aware Windows application (Excel) that AutoCAD communicates with.

▸ The DDE Topic is the filename (Sheet1) the app loads.

▸ DDE Path is the command (Excel.Exe) that launches the DDE remote app; it can include the subdirectory name.

▸ DDE Advise is a toggle that determines whether the DDE link is hot (1) or warm (0). ∎

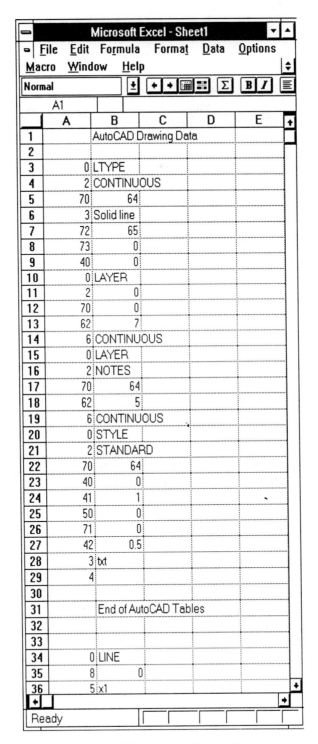

TIP NUMBER 40
Spreadsheet Won't Load

If AutoCAD is unable to load Excel via DDE, it displays the following dialogue box:

The **DDE Initiate Conversation** dialogue box gives you an opportunity to help AutoCAD find the location of the spreadsheet program on your computer's hard disk. Edit the **Command line:** text box (at the bottom of the dialogue box) with the correct DOS path.

If you are using another spreadsheet program, such as Lotus 1-2-3/W or Borland Quattro Pro for Windows, then this is the place you change AutoCAD's default of Excel.

This dialogue box also lets you toggle the DDE link between hot (the default) or warm. Leave the setting checked for now to maintain the hot link. ∎

---

display the **Task List** dialogue box (see Figure).

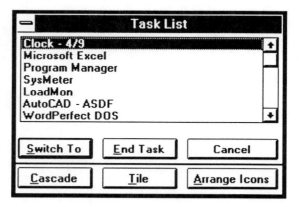

Click on the **Tile** button. Windows resizes and repositions AutoCAD and Excel so that both are the same size and shape, side-by-side (see Figure).

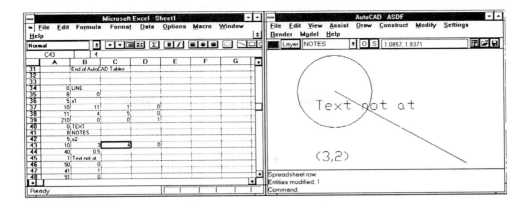

5. Make the following change in Excel and watch the change reflected in AutoCAD: Click on cell **B37**, change the 1 to an 11 and press **<Enter>**. In AutoCAD, the line's starting point zips from (1,1) to (11,1).

6. Try making some other changes. In cell **B45** change "Text at" to "Text not at".

7. To make the assertion true, change cell **B44** from 2 to 4. In AutoCAD, the text moves up by two inches.

Unfortunately, it is not as easy to make a change in AutoCAD and have it reflected in Excel. We'll see how to do that later in this chapter.

Decoding DXF

It may appear to you that the AutoCAD drawing data appearing in the Excel worksheet looks like gibberish. But there is indeed a pattern to the numbers.

First, notice that the data appears in just two columns, A and B. That indicates that the data in column B is linked to the data in column A. Everything in the DXF definition comes in pairs, as follows:

▸ Column A contains DXF *group numbers*.
▸ Column B contains DXF *data*.
▸ Sometimes the DXF data spills into columns C, D, et cetera.

Group number 0, for example, describes the start of the description of an entity.

Entities and Tables. Scan down the worksheet and look for every occurrence of a zero in column A:

```
0  LTYPE
0  LAYER
0  LAYER
0  STYLE
   End of AutoCAD Tables

0  LINE
0  TEXT
0  TEXT
0  CIRCLE
-99  End of DDE
```

The 0 indicates the start of a table (in the first half, before "*End of AutoCAD Tables*") or an entity, in the second half. The word next to each group 0 is familiar to us. When you drew the ASDF drawing, you drew a line (0 LINE), two pieces of text (0 TEXT and 0 TEXT), and a circle (0 CIRCLE). You used the default linetype (0 LTYPE), two layers (0 LAYER and 0 LAYER), and the default text style (0 STYLE).

We see that the group 0's are in two sections. An AutoCAD DWG file describes the drawing by means of (1) *tables* and (2) *entities*:

▶ **The Table Section** describes drawing resources such as layer names, text styles, linetypes, named views, viewports, named UCSs, and blocks.

▶ **The Entity Section** describes the entities that you draw—points, lines, circles, arcs, et cetera—and block insertion points.

When AutoCAD sends drawing data to Excel, the table section is always sent first—unless you tell AutoCAD not to send the table section. For the remainder of this tutorial, we refer only to the entities section.

Group 8: Layer Names. Following each group 0 is the group 8 entry that names the entity's layer. Pick out all group 8's from the worksheet, as shown below:

```
0  LINE
8     0
. . .

0  TEXT
8  NOTES
```

```
. . .
0  TEXT
8  NOTES
. . .
0  CIRCLE
8  NOTES
```

Recall that you drew the line on layer "0," while the two lines of text and the circle were drawn on layer "NOTES." Notice how the worksheet formats text as left-justified and numbers as right-justified.

Group 5: Entity Handles. Following the layer name is group 5, the hexadecimal entity handle. When you add an entity to a drawing, AutoCAD gives it a unique hexadecimal (base 16) number. Scan through for all the group 5's:

```
0  LINE
8     0
5  x1
. . .
0  TEXT
8  NOTES
5  x2
. . .
0  TEXT
8  NOTES
5  x3
. . .
0  CIRCLE
8  NOTES
62        1
5  x4
```

The four entities are assigned handle numbers 1 through 4. The *x*-prefix indicates that the number is a hexadecimal (base 16) number, rather than a decimal number.

Group 62: Colors. In the list above, the circle has an extra entry: "62   1." Group 62 refers to the entity's color number. Color number 1 is defined by AutoCAD as red. Recall that we used the Color command to set the red color of the circle.

The lines of text do not have a color group number, even though they are colored blue. Why? We defined layer "NOTES" as blue. That information is stored higher up in the table section:

```
0 LAYER  ; table section
2 NOTES  ; layer name
70  64   ; referenced data
62  5    ; color 5 (blue)
```

Group 70: Entry Toggle. In the list above, group code 70 has a value of 64. That is a toggle to indicate the table entry is referenced by at least one entity. In this case, it means there is at least one entity on layer NOTES.

This points out an important "gotcha" in decoding DXF: AutoCAD does not write all information. The blue color of the text is not explicitly stated in the entities section. Similarly, entries in the tables section may not be used by the entities section.

Groups 10, 11, 210: Coordinates. Following the description of the entity's attributes comes the entity's coordinates, as defined by group codes 10, 11, 210, and others. Let's look at the coordinates of the line we drew:

```
0 LINE
8     0
5 x1
10       1  1  0
11       4  5  0
210      0  0  1
```

Group 10 refers to the line's starting x,y,z-coordinates: 1,1,0. Group 11 refers to the line's ending x,y,z-coordinates: 4,5,0. Group 210 refers to the line's extrusion in the x-direction: 0,0,1.

Group 40: Circle Radius. Skip ahead to the circle's data:

```
0 CIRCLE
8 NOTES
62      1
5 x4
10       4  5  0
40       2
210      0  0  1
```

Group 10, in this case, refers to the circle's center x,y,z-coordinates: 4,5,0. Group 40 refers to the circle's radius: 2.

Groups 50, 51, 71, 72, 73: Text Styles. Text is a bit more complex since it has more parameters than lines and circles:

```
0   TEXT
8   NOTES
5   x2
10      3  2  0
40      0.5
1   Text at
50      0
41      1
51      0
7   STANDARD
71      0
72      0
11      0  0  0
210     0  0  1
73      0
```

The following table describes the meaning of the group codes used by text entities:

Text Group Codes

Group Code	Meaning	Value
10	X,y,z-coordinates of insertion point	3,2,0
40	Height of the text	0.5
1	The actual text	Text at
50	Rotation angle	0 degrees
41	X-scale factor	0
51	Obliquing angle	0
7	**Style name**	**STANDARD**
71	Text generation flag	0
72	Horizontal justification	0
11	X,y,z-coordinates of alignment	0,0,0
73	Vertical justification flag	0

For the style name (group code 7), you need to refer back to line 28 in the tables section to find out the name of the font file, Txt.Shx (group code 3).

Setting Up the DDE Link

Now that you have used DDE to transfer data between AutoCAD and Excel, let's take a closer look at how two programs communicate via DDE. There are three phases to DDE communications: (1) set up the communications channel; (2) send and request data and commands; (3) shut down the channel.

Different Windows programs use different commands to set up the link, send data, and execute remote commands. (Execute remote commands? Yes, it is possible for AutoCAD to execute commands in Excel and vice versa.) Naturally enough, Excel uses its macro language to execute DDE commands, while AutoCAD uses extensions to its AutoLISP programming language to execute DDE commands, defined in the file DdeLisp.Exe.

For example, to create the communications link with AutoCAD, Excel uses the Initiate command, as follows:

```
channel=initiate("autocad","nozzle")
```

where "autocad" is the DDE name of the AutoCAD for Windows application and "nozzle" is the name of the data file to open, in this case Nozzle.Dwg. After opening the DDE channel, the Initiate function returns the number of the DDE channel, which can be stored in the variable named Channel. Windows supports 16 simultaneous DDE channels.

Unfortunately, it's harder for AutoCAD to be a DDE client. Although it can open a DDE link with another Windows program and run it, the other Windows program can only run AutoCAD via an ADS application, which interrupts AutoCAD to modify the drawing. (The AutoLISP program AcadL.Exe is both client and server, since it acts as intermediary between AutoCAD, DdeLisp, and ADS applications.)

TIP NUMBER 41

DDE Name and Command Name

Don't confuse the *DDE name* and the *command name* of a program, although they can be the same. The DDE name is the name to which the application responds via Windows' DDE mechanism; the command name is the EXE or DLL name that launches the program, and can include the DOS path. "Autocad" is AutoCAD's DDE name, while "c:\acadwin\acad" is its command name.

It doesn't help that Autodesk does not use Microsoft terminology. AutoCAD's documentation refers to the DDE name as the *app name*. The data file or spreadsheet file or work file are referred to as the *topic*, in DDE terminology. ∎

Tutorial 2
Manually Creating a DDE Link

For AutoCAD to create a communications link with another Windows program takes two steps: (1) load the DdeLisp.Exe extension; (2) initiate the DDE channel.

1. Load the DdeLisp.Exe program, as follows:

```
Command: (xload "ddelisp")
"ddelisp"
```

The DdeLisp extension contains AutoLISP functions that make it easier to work the DDE.

2. Once DdeLisp is loaded, use the DDE-specific extensions to AutoLISP. AutoCAD has an **Initiate** command, just like Excel:

```
Command: (setq channel (initiate "excel" "sheet1"))
1
```

For AutoCAD's **Initiate** command to work, Excel must be already running with worksheet Sheet1.Xls already loaded. **Initiate** returns the channel number (usually channel number 1), which is stored in a variable with the **Setq** function. If the DDE channel cannot be opened (because Excel or Sheet1 are not loaded), **Initiate** returns a value of 0.

AutoCAD, in fact, has five commands for creating a DDE link, all of which are variants on the **Initialize** function:

StartApp. starts another Windows application running and loads a data file, as follows:

```
Command: (startapp "c:\\excel\\excel" "sheet1")
```

In this example code, the **Startapp** function starts the Excel program located in the C:\Excel subdirectory (if Excel is in the DOS path, you don't need to specify the path). **Startapp** also causes Excel to load the worksheet file Sheet1.Xls. **Startapp** returns 0, whether or not it is successful. Notice that you still need to use the double backslashes, instead of the DOS standard of a single backslash, because of AutoLISP.

Startapp launches Windows applications not capable of dynamic data exchange. For example, to launch the Windows Paintbrush program with a new file:

```
Command: (startapp "c:\\windows\\pbrush" "new")
```

or to launch Paintbrush and open a bitmap file:

```
Command: (startapp "c:\\windows\\pbrush"
  "c:\\windows\\chintz.bmp")
```

Be careful: the **Startapp** function can launch multiple copies of an application. Repeating the function half-a-dozen times gets you six copies of Excel or Paintbrush running!

Initiate creates the DDE communications channel, after a Windows application has already been opened, as follows:

```
Command: (setq channel (initiate "excel" "sheet1"))
1
```

In this example code, the **Initiate** function opens a communications channel with the program with the DDE name of Excel.

Here **Initiate** also causes Excel to load the worksheet file "Sheet1.Xls." "Sheet1" is the only empty worksheet filename that Excel will automatically open. To use any other filename, the worksheet file must already exist.   **Initiate** returns the DDE channel number if successful (between 1 and 16), or 0 if it can't make the link with Excel.

AppInit combines **Initialize** with **Startapp** into a single function. Appinit loads the application and the data file, and opens the DDE communications channel, as follows:

```
Command: (setq channel (appinit "excel" "sheet1"
  "c:\\excel\\excel"))
1
```

Here, **AppInit** starts the Excel program located in the C:\Excel subdirectory, opens a communications channel with the program with the DDE name of Excel, and causes Excel to load the worksheet file Sheet1.Xls.

AppInit returns the DDE channel number if successful, or 0 if it couldn't make the link with Excel.

DdeDialog (without a "ue" suffix) is the dialogue box version of **Appinit,** as follows:

```
Command: (setq channel (ddedialog))
1
```

It displays the **DDE Initiate Conversation** dialogue box, which allows you to type in the name of the application's DDE name, data file (topic), startup path and command name, and toggle the hot link (see Figure). **Ddedialog** returns the DDE channel number if successful, or 0 if it couldn't make the link with the application.

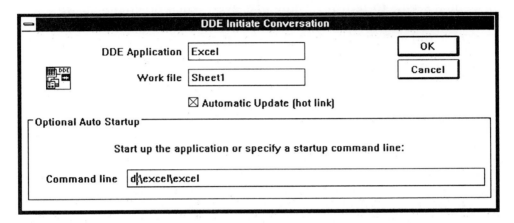

DdeDefaults and DdePrompt work together, mimicking the **AppInit** function:

```
Command: (ddedefaults "excel" "sheet1"
  "c:\\excel\\excel")
Command: (setq channel (ddeprompt))
```

DdeDefaults is a function that lets you quickly assign values to the DDE name, topic, and command name.

DdePrompt then launches the application, loads the data file (topic), and establishes the link. If the link cannot be established, it displays the **DDE Initiate Conversation** dialogue box.

Confirming the Channel Link

Once the DDE communications are established, AutoCAD has four functions to confirm the link:

ListChnls is a useful way to get a list of the channel number, DDE name and topic of the currently opened DDE channels, as follows:

```
Command: (setq numchannels (listchnls))
1 excel sheet1
1
```

ListChnls seems to return a value of 1 even when no channels are open.

GetDdeChnl, GetDdeApp, and GetDdeTopic separate out the information provided by **ListChls,** as follows:

```
Command: (setq channel (getddechannel))
1
Command: (setq ddeapp (getddeapp))
"excel"
Command: (setq topic (getddetopic))
"sheet1"
```

These three functions are the only way to get the information typed by a user in the **DDE Initiate Conversation** dialogue box.

Tutorial 3
Send a Complete Drawing

With the DDE link set up between AutoCAD and Excel, and with the link confirmed, you can try sending drawing data via DDE and the special AutoLISP commands.

1. First, though, start a new drawing; then draw a line:

   ```
   Command: line
   From point: 1,1
   To point: 4,5
   To point: <Enter>
   ```

   You will send this line from AutoCAD to the Excel worksheet.

2. Load the DdeLisp program, as follows:

   ```
   Command: (xload "ddelisp")
   "ddelisp"
   ```

3. Manually set up the DDE link, as follows:

   ```
   Command: (setq channel1 (appinit "excel" "sheet1"
      "excel"))
   1
   ```

   The AppInit function loads Excel and a worksheet with the default filename of "Sheet1.Wks." The function returns the value of "1" to confirm the link has been set up. The "1" is the number of the DDE link.

4. Now use the **SendDrawing** function to send the line data to Excel:

   ```
   Command: (setq rowcount1 (senddrawing 1))
   handles Handles are disabled
   ON/DESTROY: on
   Command:
   Spreadsheet rows: 36
   ```

The **SendDrawing** function sends everything in the drawing (tables and entities) to the spreadsheet, starting in column A of the row number you specify (row 1 in this case).

Figure: AutoCAD and Microsoft Excel windows showing Dynamic Data Exchange.

AutoCAD — QWERTY

File Edit Assist Draw Modify Display Settings
Options Utility DDE Help

Layer: 0   5.1690,0.5070

AutoCAD
****
BLOCKS
DIM:
DISPLAY
DRAW
EDIT
INQUIRY
LAYER:
MVIEW
PLOT:
SETTINGS
DDE
SURFACES
UCS:
UTILITY
ASHADE

Command: Regenerating drawing.
Command:

AutoCAD Text — QWERTY

```
Command: (appinit "excel" "sheet1" "excel")
1

Command: (setq rowcount (senddrawing 1))
handles Handles are disabled.
ON/DESTROY: on
Command:
Spreadsheet row: 36
```

Microsoft Excel - Sheet1

File Edit Formula Format Data Options Macro
Window Help

Normal

A1   0

	A	B	C	D	E	F
1	0	LTYPE				
2	2	CONTINUOUS				
3	70	64				
4	3	Solid line				
5	72	65				
6	73	0				
7	40					
8	0	LAYER				
9	2	0				
10	70	0				
11	62	7				
12	6	CONTINUOUS				
13	0	STYLE				
14	2	STANDARD				
15	70	0				
16	40					
17	41	1				
18	50	0				
19	71	0				
26						
27	0	LINE				
28	8	0				
29	5	x1				
30	10	1	1	0		
31	11	4	5	0		
32	210	0	0	1		
33						

Ready

Before sending the data, AutoCAD turns on its handles information. After
the data is sent, AutoCAD reports the number of rows (36) its data filled
in the spreadsheet (see Figure).

Tutorial 4
Receive a Complete Spreadsheet

With the drawing data in an Excel worksheet, you can change a value and send the modified data back to AutoCAD, which revises the drawing.

1. In Excel, go to cell B30 and change the line x-coordinate from 1 to 5.

2. In AutoCAD, use the **ModDrawing** command to read back in the data:

```
Command: (setq modcount2 (moddrawing channel1 1
   rowcount1 4))
Spreadsheet row:
Entities modified: 1
```

The line moves over! The **ModDrawing** function needs to know which worksheet cells to read; AutoCAD has no way to read the entire worksheet if you aren't sure which cells have changed.

Instead, start with row 1, column 1 (or column A), and extend down by the number of rows specified by variable Rowcount1 (36 rows in this example). If you have no idea how long the worksheet is, use 2048 or some other large number of rows. Move over by at least four columns. The longest Excel worksheet can be 16,384 rows longs and 256 columns wide.

You supply **ModDrawing** with parameters that specify the following:

- The starting row number, row 1 in this example
- The starting column number, 1—and not its alphabetic name, A
- The range of rows to read, 36 rows or some large number
- The range of columns to read, 4 columns

The **ModDrawing** function returns the number of entities modified. In the sample code, the value is stored in variable Modcount and is equal to 1 entity, the modified line.

The smallest range of worksheet cells you can request must include the entity name (LINE, in this example) along with the changed data. In this example, you would need to start at row 27, column 2 (B), read down 5 rows, and read over two columns, as follows:

```
Command: (setq modcount2 (moddrawing 27 2 5 2))
Spreadsheet row:
Entities modified: 1
```

Send Part of a Drawing

Instead of sending the entire drawing (complete with table information) over to Excel, you are more likely to send part of the drawing, or even just a single entity. AutoCAD has three commands for doing just that:

▸ **EntPokeCell** sends a single drawing entity to a specified location in the spreadsheet

▸ **PokeSet** sends all drawing entities in a selection set to a specified location in the spreadsheet

▸ **PokeAll** sends all drawing entities following a specified entity to a specified location in the spreadsheet

Before you can use any of these functions, you need to create a selection set:

▸ For **EntPokeCell** and **PokeAll,** use the AutoLISP function EntSel

▸ For **PokeSet,** use the SsGet function.

The format of the **EntPokeCell** function is:

```
(entpokecell channel ename startrow startcell)
```

The four required parameters are, as follows:

▸ **Channel** is the channel number that you previously opened, typically channel 1 stored in a variable with a name such as Channel1.

▸ **Ename** is the name of the entity that you acquired with EntSel, typically 60000034 (or some similar number) stored in variable with a name such as Ename1.

▸ **Startrow** is the number of the starting row where the data should be placed in the spreadsheet. To ensure data is not overwritten, use a variable with a name such as Rowcount1 to keep track of rows in Excel. Incremented the row number by one row with the **1+** function:

```
(setq rowcount1 (1+ rowcount1))
```

▸ **Startcol** is the number—not letter—of the starting column where the data should be placed in the spreadsheet. In most cases, this will be column 1.

The **PokeSet** function returns the number of spreadsheet rows filled with data. The format of the **PokeSet** function is identical with EntPokeCell:

```
(pokeset channel ename startrow startcell)
```

The **PokeAll** function returns the number of spreadsheet rows filled with data. The format of the **PokeAll** function is identical with EntPokeCell:

```
(pokeall channel ename startrow startcell)
```

Let's take a look at how the three functions work.

Tutorial 5
Send A Single Entity

First use **EntPokeCell** to send just the circle to the worksheet, as follows:

1. Add a circle to the drawing of the line, as follows:

   ```
   Command: circle
   3P/2P/<Center point>: 1,5
   Diameter/<Radius>: 1.25
   ```

2. Pick the circle with the **EntSel** function, as follows:

   ```
   Command: (setq ent1 (entsel))
   Select object: <pick the circle>
   (<Entity name: 60000034> (2.20158 4.70876 0,0))
   ```

   The **EntSel** function returns two pieces of information: (1) the entity name 60000034 and (2) the coordinates of the pick point (2.20158 4.70876 0,0).

3. Of the two, you only need the entity name, which is 60000034 (it may have a different number in your drawing). Extract the entity name with the AutoLISP **Car** function and store the name in variable Ename1, as follows:

   ```
   Command: (setq ename1 (car ent1))
   <Entity name: 60000034>
   ```

4. Now send just the circle data to the Excel worksheet with the **EntPokeCell** function, as follows:

   ```
   Command:  (setq  rowcount2  (entpokecell  channel1
   ename1 (1+
     rowcount1) 1))
   6
   ```

   The circle data should show up in the Excel worksheet below the line data. The **1+** function increments variable Rowcount1 to ensure the circle data doesn't overwrite the line data.

Tutorial 6
Send A Selection Set

Now use the **PokeSet** function to send a selection set to Excel. In this tutorial, the selection set consists of text.

1. First, add two lines of text to the drawing on layer Notes, as follows:

```
Command: layer
?/Make/.../Thaw: m
New layer name <0>: notes
?/Make/.../Thaw: <Enter>

Command: dtext
Justify/Style/<Start point>: cen
of <pick circle>
Height <0.2000>: 0.5
Rotation angle <0>: <Enter>
Text: Text at <Enter>
Text: (1,5) <Enter>
Text: <Enter>
```

2. Create a selection set of the two lines of text with the **SsGet** function, as follows:

```
Command: (setq ename2 (ssget))
Select object: c
First point: <pick point>
Other point: <window the two lines of text>
2 found Select objects: <Enter>
<Selection set: 1>
```

The **SsGet** function returns the selection set number, 1. AutoCAD Release 11 allows you to create up to six selection sets; Release 12 allows up to 256 selection sets.

3. Now send the text data to the Excel worksheet with the **PokeSet** function, as follows:

```
Command: (setq rowcount3 (pokeset channel1 ename2
    (+ 1 rowcount1 rowcount2) 1))
Spreadsheet row: 30
```

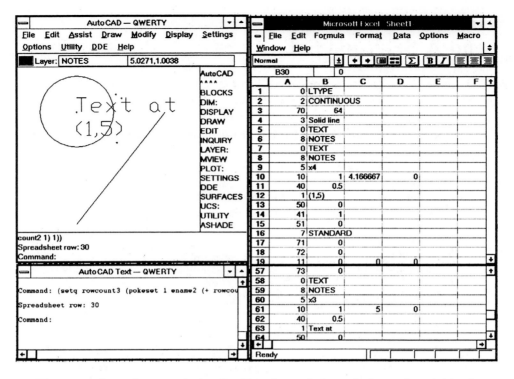

The text data shows up in the Excel worksheet below the circle data. Note that the data appears in reverse order: the second line of text comes first (see Figure).

Tutorial 7
Send All Following Entities

The **PokeAll** function sends all entities beginning with a selected entity. That makes it easy to send the most recently created entities to the spreadsheet. When you begin with the first entity in the drawing, then the **PokeAll** function is equivalent to the **SendDrawing** function.

1. You reuse the data from the previous two examples to try out **PokeAll,** as follows:

```
Command: (setq rowcount4 (pokeall channel1 ename1
   (1+ rowcount1) 1))
37
```

2. The circle and text data should show up in the Excel worksheet below the previous text. Since variable Ename1 contained the entity number of the circle, the circle and all entities following the circle (the two lines of text) are sent to the worksheet, beginning with row 40, column 1.

Sending Table Information

To send a block, or layer information or a linetype definition, to Excel, you send tables, rather than entities. *Tables* is Autodesk's term for the drawing information that describes named features, such as blocks, layers, viewports, and linetypes. AutoCAD for Windows has three functions for sending table information to a spreadsheet:

▸ **PokeAllTbl** sends all table information in the drawing to a specified location in the spreadsheet.

▸ **PokeTblCell** sends a specific table to a specific location in the spreadsheet.

▸ **PokeTbl** is like PokeTblCell but is meant for applications other than spreadsheets.

Under Windows, AutoCAD sends table data shown in the following Table:

Tables Sent Via DDE

Table	DDE Number	DXF Name
Viewports	0	VPORT
Linetypes	1	LTYPE
Layer names	2	LAYER
Text styles	3	STYLE
View names	4	VIEW
Named UCS	5	UCS
Named blocks	6	BLOCK

Note that AutoCAD for Windows does not send the AppId (application ID numbers) and DimStyle (dimension styles tables).

Tutorial 8
Send All Table Data

The **PokeAllTbl** sends all of the table information in the drawing to the spreadsheet. The function takes three parameters:

▸ The DDE channel number

▸ The starting row and cell where the information should be placed in the spreadsheet

1. Ensure that the DDE link exists between AutoCAD and Excel.

2. Use the **PokeAllTbl** function, as follows:

```
Command: (pokealltbl channel1 1 1)
Spreadsheet row: 36
```

The table data should appear in the Excel worksheet, beginning with row 1, column 1. The **PokeAllTbl** function returns the number of worksheet rows filled, 36 in this example.

Tutorial 9
Sending Specific Table Data

The **PokeTblCell** function sends one specific set of table data in the drawing to the spreadsheet. The function takes four parameters:

- The DDE channel number

- The starting row and cell where the information should be placed in the spreadsheet

- The table number

1. To send layer data (table 2) via the **PokeAllTbl** function, type the following:

   ```
   Command: (poketblcell channel1 100 1 2)
   15
   ```

2. The layer data should appear in the Excel worksheet, beginning with row 100, column 1. The **PokeTblCell** function returns the number of filled rows, 15 here.

PokeTbl is a generalized function meant to work with applications other than spreadsheets.

Receiving Table Information

To get back modified table information, you use the **ModDrawing** function just as you do with drawing entity data. Since the **ModDrawing** function requires a range of cells, AutoCAD comes with a couple of additional functions to determine the number of rows used by table data:

- **LenAllTbl** finds out the number of rows used by all table information in the spreadsheet.

- **LenTbl** finds out the number of rows used by a specific named table.

(I find it strange that AutoCAD has no equivalent functions to find the number of rows used by entity data.)

Tutorial 10
Receiving All Table Data

To get back all the table information, use the **ModDrawing** function together with **LenAllTbl** function.

1. Ensure that DDE links AutoCAD and Excel.

2. Use the **LenAllTbl** function to find the length of the tables section in the spreadsheet, as follows:

   ```
   Command: (setq rownumber1 (lenalltbl))
   32
   ```

   The tables section takes up 32 rows. The value is stored in variable RowNumber1.

3. Use the **ModDrawing** function to retrieve the table data, as follows:

   ```
   Command: (moddrawing 1 1 rownumber1 4)
   Entities modified:
   ```

The **LenAllTbl** function returns the number of rows filled by table data in the worksheet (32 in the example above) and stored in the variable Rownumber1. The **ModDrawing** function uses this number to just update the table information in the current drawing.

Tutorial 11
Receiving Partial Table Data

To get back specific table information, such as a modified layer name, use the **LenTbl** function.

1. Use the **LenTbl** function to find the location of the layer table, which is table 2, as follows:

   Command: **(setq rownumber2 (lentbl 2))**
   15

   The **LenTbl** function reports that the table 2 (layers) takes up 15 rows in the Excel worksheet.

2. Now use the **ModDrawing** function to retrieve the layer tables from Excel, as follows:

   Command: **(moddrawing 1 1 rownumber2 4)**

The value of 2 tells the **LenTbl** function to look for all layer information in the spreadsheet. **LenTbl** returns the number of rows filled by layer table data in the spreadsheet (15 in the example above) and stored in the variable Rownumber2. The **ModDrawing** function uses this number to update the table information in the current drawing.

After the drawing tables have been updated, you may need to perform a regen in order to see the changes to the drawing.

Terminating the DDE Link

You terminate the DDE link simply by exiting Excel or AutoCAD. In either case, Windows will let you know that a link exists and asks if you want to exit anyhow (see Figure).

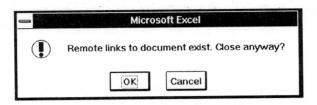

To terminate a specific link from within AutoCAD, use the **Terminate** function, specifying the DDE channel to terminate, as follows:

```
Command: (terminate "excel" "sheet1" channel1)
0
```

You must specify the DDE name, topic, and channel number. To terminate all DDE links from within AutoCAD, use the **DdeDone** function, as follows:

```
Command: (ddedone)
1
```

This sends the terminate message to all remote applications, shuts down the Windows DDE function, and frees up the memory used by the DDE process.

Summary

In this chapter, you learned about dynamic data exchange and how it works with AutoCAD for Windows. In the next chapter, you learn about programming with Visual Basic.

Introduction to Visual Basic

*I*t could be the most intriguing aspect to Release 12
for Windows: the ability to interface AutoCAD with a
lowcost programming environment called Visual Basic.
While Visual Basic does not have the power to replace
C-based ADS programming, Visual Basic excels at effortless
creation of user interfaces for add-on software. This chapter
introduces Visual Basic and describes how it works.

Executive Summary

Visual Basic is a programming language that combines original Basic's ease-of-learning with today's object-oriented, event-driven programming paradigm. AutoCAD Releases 11 and 12 support Visual Basic 1 and 2, respectively, via DDE.

To write a Visual Basic program, you work with subroutines—that all. There are three steps to creating a subroutine:

- Define the subroutine
- Write the subroutine code
- End the subroutine

Visual Basic 2 supports 33 kinds of events, ranging from Click (pressing the button on the mouse) to Resize, the change in size of a window. To link a subroutine with an event, use the **subr_event** construction:

- **Subr** is the name of the subroutine
- **Event** is the name of the event, such as a mouse click
- The underscore (_) links the subroutine with the event

Visual Basic 2 supports 171 properties of objects in a program, ranging from BackColor (the background color) to TwipsPerPixelX, the size of an object. To link a property with an object, use the **obj_prop** construction:

- **Obj** is the name of the object, such as a dialogue box
- **Prop** is the name of the property, such as text
- The period (.) links the object with the property

AutoCAD Release 11 includes a sample Visual Basic application called "VbAcad." Applications written with Visual Basic 1 require the VbRun100.Dll runtime dynamic link library, supplied with AutoCAD Release 11.

AutoCAD Release 12 includes a sample Visual Basic application called "Asvu." Applications written with Visual Basic 2 require the VbRun200.Dll runtime dynamic link library, supplied with AutoCAD Release 12.

Programming in AutoCAD

AutoLISP was added to AutoCAD in 1985, first in v2.15 as an undocumented feature, then in v2.17 to help third-party developers create more sophisticated menu macros. By the time AutoCAD v2.5 came out a year later, AutoLISP had evolved into a full-fledged programming language that could access drawing entity data. AutoLISP quickly surpassed menu macros as the most popular way to customize AutoCAD.

The reasons for AutoLISP's popularity are clear: it is powerful, it is easy to learn, it is tightly integrated with AutoCAD, and—most important—it is free. AutoLISP does have its drawbacks: it is relatively slow, it lacks random file access, and—most important—lacks a development environment.

For programmers, the development environment is critical to productivity. AutoLISP lacks an integrated editor, syntax checker (important for checking those troublesome parentheses), linker, and compiler. The alternative to AutoLISP, the ADS (AutoCAD development system), is too expensive in the DOS version and—in any case—is not integrated.

The Windows environment creates *de facto* integration. You quickly move from any Windows-based text editor to compiler to debugging under AutoCAD. Visual Basic is a tool for creating applications that interact with AutoCAD and that look and feel like a real Windows application.

What is Basic?

William Gates, founder of Microsoft, got his start as a teenage programmer, cocreating a version of the Basic programming language for the Altair computer, one of the very first personal computers sold as a kit in the mid-seventies. *Basic* is the acronym for beginner's all-purpose symbolic instruction code. Basic was invented at Dartmouth College as a simple way to program computers. Almost all personal computers include a version of Basic.

When IBM began designing its first PC in 1980, it built a version of the Basic programming language into the computer's ROM (read-only memory). If you started the computer without a bootable floppy disk inserted in its disk drive, the computer loaded Cassette Basic instead of PC-DOS (personal computer disk-based operating system). Cassette Basic was named for its ability to save and load files from an ordinary cassette recorder. Both the Basic programming language and the PC-DOS operating system were written by Microsoft.

Bundled in with the PC-DOS v1.0 operating system was an advanced version of Cassette Basic, called BasicA (short for Advanced Basic). Microsoft also offered it under its own brand name of GW-Basic. The GW stood for "gee-whiz" (or "Gates, William" for the conspiracy-minded) and did gee-whiz things like draw graphics and sound notes on the PC's speaker.

During the mid-eighties, the Basic programming language languished as other, more powerful programming languages—such as Pascal and C—took over the hearts and minds of programmers. But Microsoft didn't forget its roots and began marketing a new and improved version of Basic, called QuickBasic. It came with some of the bells and whistles that modern programming languages must have: an integrated programming environment and a high-speed compiler to produce stand-alone programs.

When MS-DOS v5.0 was released in 1990, Microsoft included an interpreted-version of QuickBasic. To replace it in the marketplace, Microsoft had Visual Basic.

What is Visual Basic?

Visual Basic has two distinct features setting it apart from other versions of Basic—indeed, from many other programming languages: (1) Visual Basic is event-driven and (2) Visual Basic has Windows GUI tools.

Unfortunately, Autodesk has limited Visual Basic to being a "front-end" to AutoCAD. That means it cannot be tightly integrated into the AutoCAD environment as can a C-based ADS application. Still, you can have Visual Basic send AutoLISP and ADS constructs, as well as regular AutoCAD commands, via DDE.

Event-driven. When you use a program written for Microsoft Windows, you are using an *event-driven program*. To understand the meaning of event driven, let's contrast event-driven programs with traditional CLI (command-line interface) programs, such as AutoCAD. AutoCAD waits at the Command: prompt for you to type in a command, such as Line. When you press <Enter> after Line, AutoCAD checks the word "LINE" against the list of commands it knows about. If it finds LINE, AutoCAD branches to the program code that executes the Line command.

An event-driven program waits for an event to occur, such as the press of a mouse button, the press of an <Enter> or <Tab> key, or the passage of time. If the program sees that there is a command associated with the position of the cursor, it executes the command sequence.

Windows GUI. The Windows graphical user interface is instantly recognizable with its check boxes, option buttons, scroll bars, frames, and list boxes; it lets you display two or more application programs on the screen at once and even run more than one program at a time.

Visual Basic includes a set of tools that lets you add a Windows-like GUI interface to your application program. Creating the GUI interface is as easy as using a drawing program: you just pick the feature you want (option button, scroll bar, whatever), place it and size it, then associate code with it. No graphics programming ability is required to produce something that looks like a professionally written Windows program.

The Basics of Event-Driven Programming

To learn event-driven programming with Visual Basic, it is helpful to understand regular Basic or another programming language—even AutoLISP. But that's where the similarity ends.

In other programming languages, you have a main piece of code that calls subroutines. In AutoLISP, it looks like this:

```
(defun subroutine1 ()
  ; code here
)

(defun subroutine2 ()
  ; more code here
)

(defun c:progname ()
  (subroutine 1)
  (subroutine 2)
)
```

If you are more familiar with Pascal, you'll recognize that the program is typical formatted like this:

```
program progname;

function subroutine1;
begin
  (* code here *)
end;

function subroutine2;
begin
  (* more code here *)
end;

begin
  subroutine1;
```

```
    subroutine2;
end.
```

And if you're a C programmer, you know that the main part actually is called "main," as follows:

```
main()
{
  subroutine1;
  subroutine2;
}

subroutine1;
{
  /* code here */
}

subroutine2;
{
  /* more code here */
}
```

All three of these "traditional" programming languages have a single main part of the code where the program begins. Its primary purpose is to call subroutines.

In Visual Basic, you throw away the notion of a main code. There is no all-encompassing AutoLISP-style "(defun())", there is no Pascal-like "program" and there is no C "main()". Instead, all code in Visual Basic exists in subroutines collected together as a *project*, as follows:

```
sub display1_click()
  'code here
end sub

sub factorial ()
  'more code here
end sub
```

There is no beginning or end defined in the code. The "subroutines" are collected together by name in a *project* file. When the program runs, each subroutine waits for something to occur; each subroutine reacts to an event in its own way. For example, subroutine Display1_Click() reacts to the user pressing the mouse button when the cursor is located over the **OK** button. Subroutine Factorial() is more like the traditional subroutine; it is referenced by other subroutines to calculate the factorial of a number.

Programming with Visual Basic

Naturally, you can use Visual Basic to write traditional-style subroutines that perform tasks such as calculating the factorial of a number. Any programming language does that, even AutoLISP. The power behind Visual Basic is that it: (1) links events with subroutines and (2) links objects with properties.

Here is a description of the three parts that make up a Visual Basic subroutine and how they permit event-driven programming:

1. Define the subroutine
2. Write the subroutine code
3. End the subroutine

Define a Subroutine. Visual Basic links an event with a subroutine by the underscore character (_). It's that simple.

For example, you've given a text box the name of "Display1." You want the user to be able to edit the contents of the text box when the user clicks the mouse button on the text box. You link the text box to the click event with the following format:

```
sub display1_click ()
```

Let's examine the meaning of each word in this line of code:

- The word "sub" defines a subroutine called "display1_click()."

- The name before the underscore, "display1," is the name of the GUI object, in this case a text box given the name "display1" (you see how that happens later in this chapter).

- The underscore (_) links the GUI object with an event.

- The name after the underscore, "click," defines the action. Visual Basic calls actions "events" and defines the press of the mouse button as a "click" event.

Triggering the event makes the subroutine leap into action. When the cursor is on top of the text box and when you click the mouse button, the subroutine executes.

Using the underscore makes it easy to define several events with each GUI object. For example, you may want to define what happens when the user uses the keyboard to move to the text box, usually by pressing the **<Tab>** key. Visual Basic calls this changing the "focus" to the text box.

Thus you would have two subroutines, as follows:

```
sub display1_click ()
  ; code here
end sub

sub display1_gotfocus ()
  ; same code here
end sub
```

Visual Basic supports dozens of events, although not all events apply to all situations. For example, it makes sense to click on a button but it doesn't make sense to drag a button. Visual Basic v1 supports 25 events, as follows:

```
Change, Click
DblClick, DragDrop, DragOver, DropDown
GotFocus
KeyDown, KeyPress, KeyUp,
LinkClose, LinkError, LinkExecute, LinkOpen, Load,
LostFocus
MouseDown, MouseMove, MouseUp
Paint, PathChange, PatternChange
Resize
Timer
Unload
```

Visual Basic v2 supports eight additional events, as follows:

```
Activate
Deactivate
LinkNotify
QueryUnload
RowColChange
Scroll, SetChange
Updated
```

Write the Subroutine Code. When you click on the text box, Visual Basic activates the subroutine. What happens depends on how you write the subroutine. It could display a message, change the property of the text box, or find the factorial of a number.

The power behind Visual Basic code is that it links *objects* with *properties* by a simple period character (.). A property is the attribute of an object. For example, some of the properties of a text box are its color, its location on the screen, its size, and whether or not it is displayed.

On-Line Help for Visual Basic

The easiest way to find the meaning of event names and other items is to read Visual Basic's excellent on-line help (see Figure).

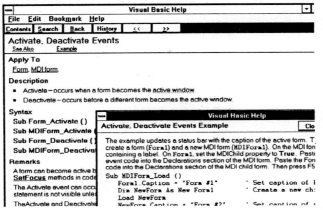

Click on the green underlined "Example" and Help displays sample code that you can copy into your Visual Basic code. ■

For example, to make the text in the Display1 text box show the message "Error, try again.", use the format:

```
display1.text="Error: Try again."
```

This line of code defines what happens when you click on the text box. Lets look at the three parts:

- The name before the period, "display1," determines which object to act upon. In this case, the user clicks on the text box and the subroutine acts upon the text box.

- The period (.) links the object (display1) with the property, text.

- The name after the period, "text," determines which property to change. In this case, the subroutine changes the text in the text box to display the words "Error, try again."

Visual Basic provides nearly two hundred properties. As with events, not all properties apply to all objects. The 89 properties supported by Visual Basic v1 are:

```
ActiveControl,    ActiveForm,    Alignment,    Archive,
AutoRedraw, AutoSize
BackColor, BorderStyle
Cancel,   Caption,   Checked,   ControlBox,   CtlName,
CurrentX, CurrentY,
Default,  DragIcon,  DragMode,  DrawMode,  DrawStyle,
DrawWidth, Drive
Enabled
FileName, FillColor, FillStyle, FontBold, FontCount,
FontItalic, FontName, Fonts, FontSize, FontStrikethru,
FontTransparent, FontUnderline, ForeColor, FormName,
hDC, Height, Hidden, hWnd
Icon, Image, Index, Interval
LargeChange, Left, LinkItem, LinkMode, LinkTimeout,
LinkTopic, List, ListCount, ListIndex
Max,   MaxButton,   Min,   MinButton,   MousePointer,
MultiLine
Normal
Page, Parent, Path, Pattern, Picture
ReadOnly
ScaleHeight,   ScaleLeft,   ScaleMode,   ScaleTop,
ScaleWidth, ScrollBars, SelLength, SelStart, SelText,
SmallChange, Sorted, Style, System
TabIndex, TabStop, Tag, Text, Top
Value, Visible
Width, WindowState.
```

Version 2 supports an additional 82 properties. as follows:

Action, Archive

BackStyle, BorderColor, BorderWidth

CellSelected, Class, ClipControls, Clip, ColAlignment, Col, Cols, Columns, ColWidth, Color

Data, DataText

Execute, ExeName

FileNumber, FixedAlignment, FixedCols, FixedRow, Focus, Format

GridLines

HelpContextId, HelpFile, HideSelection, HideLight, HostName

ItemData, KeyPreview, LeftCol, IpOleObject

MaxLength, MdiChild, MultiSelect

Name, NewIndex

PasswordChar, PasteOk, PrevInstance, Protocol

RowHeight, Row, Rows
Selected, SelEndCol, SelEndRow, ServerAcceptFormatsCount,
ServerAcceptFormats, ServerClassCount, ServerClassesDisplay,
ServerClasses, ServerClass, ServerGetFormatsCount, ServerGetFormats,
ServerProtocolCount, ServerProtocol, ServerShow, ServerType,
ServerVerbsCount, ServerVerbs, Shape, Shortcut, SourceDoc, Stretch
TimeOut, Title, TopIndex, TopRow, TwipsPerPixelX, TwipsPerPixelY
UpdateOptions
Verb
WindowList, WordWrap
X1, X2
Y1, Y2

Visual Basic v2 makes it easy to know the properties supported by an
object. The **Window | Properties** command displays the **Properties**
dialogue box (see Figure above). It lists the default values of the currently
selected object and lets you make changes.

End the Subroutine. Finally, to end the subroutine, Visual Basic supplies
the words:

```
End sub
```

In Visual Basic, you gather all the subroutines into a single project. You
never see all the code at once, as you do in other programming languages.
Instead, you only see the one subroutine you are currently working with.
Let's see how that works in the tutorial that follows.

TIP NUMBER 45
What's a Twip?

Check Visual Basic's on-line help to find out the properties of a specific object.
For example: *TwipsPerPixelY*.

From Help, you learn that a *twip* is logical unit of measure used in design
screens. It is similar in concept to Hewlett-Packard's *plu*, a plotter unit. There are
1440 twips to the inch, which comes from 20 twips to the typesetter's point (there
are 72 points to the inch). ∎

Tutorial 1
Trying Out a Visual Basic Application

Now that you have been introduced to event-driven programming, try running the sample Visual Basic program supplied with AutoCAD for Windows.

If you have Release 11, the sample program provided is called VbAcad.Exe and is found in the \AcadWin\Ads\Win subdirectory. If you have Release 12, the sample program provided is called Asvu.Exe and is found in the \AcadWin\Vb\Asvu subdirectory.

Release 11: Running VbAcad.Exe.   The VbAcad program creates a floating menu of AutoCAD tools (see Figure). When you click on a button, the Visual Basic code sends a command to AutoCAD via DDE. When you click on the button labelled "LINE," the Vbacad.Exe program sends the Line command to AutoCAD. Here's how to use the VbAcad program:

1. Start AutoCAD.

2. Start Vbacad.Exe with the **Run** command. In the Program Manager,

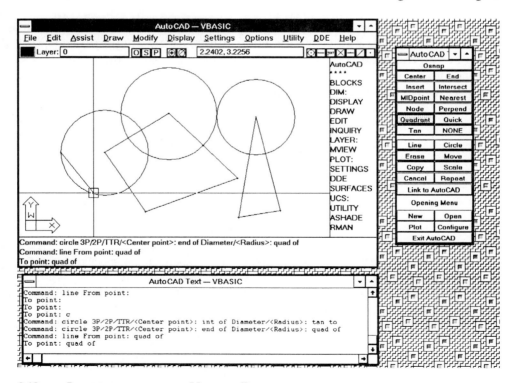

select **File** from the menu bar, pick **Run**, then type in "\acadwin-\ads\win\vbacad.exe"). Finally, pick the **OK** button.

3. Size the AutoCAD window so that you have room on your computer screen to display both AutoCAD and VbAcad's AutoCAD Toolbox (see Figure). Move VbAcad's AutoCAD Toolbox beside AutoCAD but not on top of it. (If you place VbAcad on top AutoCAD, VbAcad disappears the next time you click on the AutoCAD screen.)

4. Try using the Vbacad AutoCAD Toolbox. Pick the **New** button to start a new drawing. The buttons under "Opening Menu" only work at the Main Menu.

5. Pick the **Line** button to begin drawing a line. Pick the **Circle** button to draw circles. Pick the **Repeat** button to repeat the last command.

6. Try using some of the object snap buttons, such as **End** and **Quad** in the middle of the drawing and editing commands.

VbAcad.Exe and its support files are located in the \Acadwin\Ads\Win subdirectory:

- ► VbAcad.Exe is the compiled (*Exe*cutable) program

- ► VbAcad.Bas contains the *Bas*ic source code

- ► VbAcad.Mak is the project *Mak*e file that keeps track of the code and forms

- ► VbAcad.Frm describes the *Form* (the GUI interface)

Release 12: Running Asvu.Exe. The Asvu program creates a dialogue box that lets you view and change many of AutoCAD's nearly 200 system variables (see Figure). Asvu is short for AutoCAD System Variable Utility.

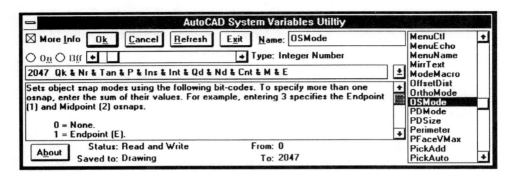

You select a system variable name from the list box on the far right. The dialogue box communicates with AutoCAD via DDE to find out the current value of the system variable. The dialogue box also tells you the allowable range of variables; when you make a change, the Asvu program instructs AutoCAD to change. Here's how to use the Asvu program:

1. Move the AcadVb.Dll dynamic link library from \Acadwin to the \Acadwin\Vb\Asvu subdirectory, otherwise Asvu will not run.

2. Start AutoCAD.

3. Load the ADS application DdeBas.Exe, as follows:

    ```
    Command: (xload "ddebas")
    ```

4. Start Asvu.Exe with the **Run** command. In the Program Manager, select **File** from the menu bar, pick **Run**, then type in "\Acadwin\Vb-\Asvu.Exe". Finally, pick the **OK** button.

5. Size the AutoCAD window so that you have room on your computer screen to display both AutoCAD and Asvu's dialogue box.

6. Try using the Asvu dialogue box. Pick a system variable from the list box, such as OsMode (short for object snap mode). Asvu interrogates AutoCAD and displays the current value, along with all permissible values.

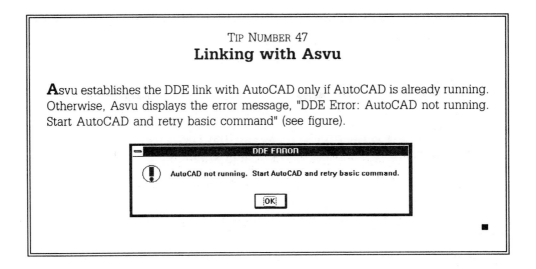

TIP NUMBER 47
Linking with Asvu

Asvu establishes the DDE link with AutoCAD only if AutoCAD is already running. Otherwise, Asvu displays the error message, "DDE Error: AutoCAD not running. Start AutoCAD and retry basic command" (see figure).

7. Use the horizontal scroll bar to change the value of OsMode. Click on the **OK** button to send the new OsMode value to AutoCAD.

8. You can make the dialogue box smaller by clicking on the **More Info** check box in the upper left corner (see Figure).

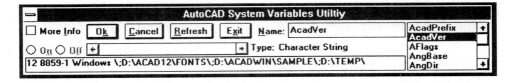

9. Exit the dialogue box by clicking on the **Exit** button.

10. To free the memory used by DdeBas.Exe, use the Xunload function, as follows:

```
Command: (xunload "ddebas")
```

Asvu.Exe and its support files are located in the \Acadwin\Vb subdirectory:

- ▸ Asvu.Exe is the compiled (*Exe*cutable) program

- ▸ Maint.Bas contains the *Bas*ic source code

- AdsFuncs.Bas contains the source code of AutoCAD's ADS functions common to all Visual Basic applications

- Global.Bas contains source code that defines ADS data types

- Internal.Bas contains additional source code

- SysVars.Mak is the project *Make* file that keeps track of the code and forms

- SysVars.Frm describes the *Form* (the GUI interface)

- AboutBox.Frm describes the **About** dialogue box

- AdsFuncs.Frm, an invisible form, contains ADS functions common to all Visual Basic applications

Although you ran an EXE file, Visual Basic EXE files are not truly stand-alone. Like the old CBasic (compiled Basic) programming language, Visual Basic needs an additional run-time module to be present. Version 1 needs Vbrun100.Dll, while version 2 needs Vbrun200.Dll. This dynamic link library is supplied with Visual Basic; AutoCAD Release 11 provides Vbrun100.Dll, while Release 12 provides Vbrun200.Dll. If you intend to distribute Visual Basic programs, make sure you include a copy of Vbrun100.Dll or Vbrun200.Dll, otherwise your software will not run.

Summary

In this chapter, you were introduced to Visual Basic and the concept of event-driven programming. You learned about linking events and properties to objects. Finally, you loaded and ran the Visual Basic application supplied with AutoCAD.

In the next chapter, you learn how to program in Visual Basic by examining the code, rearranging the Asvu program's user interface, and then writing your own code.

15

Visual Basic Programming

The last chapter introduced Visual Basic and how its event-driven programming differs from traditional programming languages. This chapter introduces you to methods of programming in Visual Basic. You look at the code in Asvu.Exe, then modify its GUI user interface, and finally look at the code that lets the Visual Basic application communicate with AutoCAD.

Examining in the Code

Now that you've had a chance to let a Visual Basic program carry out AutoCAD commands by "remote control," let's take a look at the GUI and the code making up Asvu.Exe. I assume that you have Visual Basic 2 installed on your computer. Start Visual Basic by double-clicking on its icon in the Program Manager. The Figure shows some of the components of the Visual Basic programming environment:

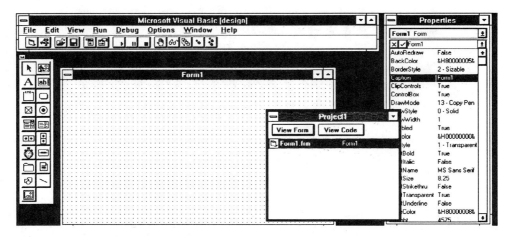

- ► Along the top is the menu bar with 14 icon buttons

- ► At the right is the 36-icon tool palette, which contains the component parts for creating custom GUIs

- ► In the center is a blank form, named "Form1," ready for you to create the custom GUI

- ► In the lower-right is the **Project** dialogue box, with a number of pre-loaded VDX (virtual device driver) modules

- ► In the upper right is the **Properties** dialogue box, which lists all properties that apply to the currently-selected object, along with default values

- ► Click on **Window | Color Palette** to bring up the color and texture palette, which floats at the bottom of the screen

- ► When you run a program, the Debug window shows up on the screen

Tutorial 1
Loading a Project File

The project file contains the names of all files needed by Visual Basic. It is named *project file* because it defines the programming project. It's also known as the "make" file after its extension, *.Mak. To work with Asvu, you open its project file, SysVars.Mak, as follows:

1. On the Visual Basic menu bar, click on **File**, then select **Open Project...**.

2. When the dialogue box appears, click on directory names until you get to the \Acadwin\Vb subdirectory.

3. Double-click on the SysVars.Mak filename to load the files in the Asvu project. The **SysVars.Mak** dialogue box displays the seven files used by Asvu (see Figure).

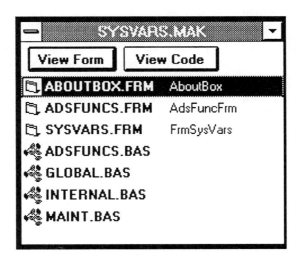

Tip Number 48
The Transparent Background

Visual Basic has a transparent background. You may find it visually less confusing if you minimize the Program Manager and all other applications to icon size. ■

Examining the Visual Basic Files

There are two kinds of files used by Asvu: (1) FRM form files and (2) BAS code files. Those are the two kinds of files you create with Visual Basic programs. The FRM form files describe the user interface and the code attached to each element of the interface; BAS files contain only code.

Notice the two buttons at the top of the dialogue box: **View Form** and **View Code**. They correspond to the two kinds of files listed in the dialogue box: *.Frm and *.Bas.

With the down-arrow cursor key, move down the list of files. When the cursor reaches a BAS file, the **View Form** button grays out, proving that BAS files contain no GUI code.

View Form. The view form defines the look and feel of a Visual Basic program. *Form* is Visual Basic's name for the graphical user interface, the part of the program that the user sees and interacts with. Think of the word "form" in the context of filling out a credit application form, which poses questions whose answers you fill in. You can get a feel for how the Asvu GUI fits together, as follows:

1. **View a Form.** In the **SysVars.Mak** project dialogue box, double-click on the filename SysVars.Frm, then click on the **View Form** button. This loads the "AutoCAD System Variables Utiltiy" [*sic*] form, which is the graphical user interface to the Asvu program (see Figure).

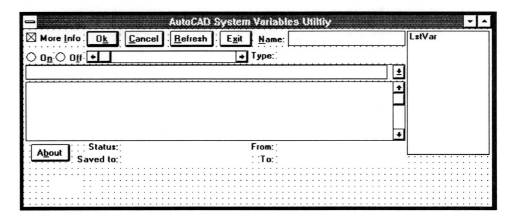

2. **Select an Object.** Click on one of the objects, such as the box labelled **LstVar** at the extreme right. (The purpose of the **LstVar** list box is to list the names of AutoCAD system variables.) Immediately, it is surrounded by eight small black squares. These are called *sizing handles*

and let you move and size the button, much like grips in AutoCAD Release 12 (see Figure).

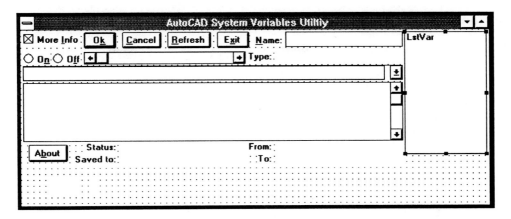

3. **Sizing Handles.** Move the cursor to one of the sizing handles, such as the one in the lower right of the LstVar list box. Notice how the cursor changes to a double-ended arrow.

4. **Size the Object.** Click on the sizing handle and drag the corner in any direction. The LstVar list box changes proportions, gets larger and smaller as you move the mouse around.

5. **Move the Object.** To move the list box, click on the center of the LstVar box and hold the mouse button down, then drag it around. You can relocate the box anywhere on the form.

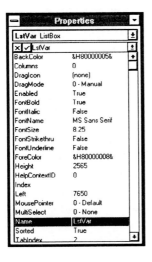

6. **View the Object's Properties.** Finally, click on the **Properties** dialogue box, which is probably hiding underneath the other windows. It lists all the properties of the **LstVar** list box (see Figure).

As you have seen from the **LstVar** list box, it is very easy to modify the user interface of an existing Visual Basic application. You simply move and resize the objects with the mouse—much easier than writing code to create the user interface, as with AutoCAD's own DCL (dialogue control language).

View Code. Now take a look at the BASIC programming code behind the list box. In the **AutoCAD System Variables Utiltiy** dialogue box, double-click on the **LstVar** list box. Visual Basic displays the **SysVars.Frm** dialogue box (see Figure).

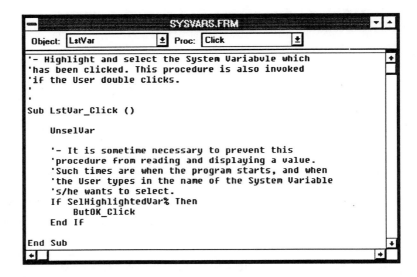

The code you see shows what happens when you click on the LstVar list box. Here is what it looks like with comments stripped out:

```
Sub LstVar_Click()
   UnselVar
   If SelHighlightedVar% Then
      ButOK_Click
   End If
End Sub
```

Let's examine the meaning of each line:

▸ From the previous chapter, you know that the LstVar_Click subroutine links the LstVar list box with the click operation.

▸ The function **UnselVar** unselects the currently selected AutoCAD system variable. UnselVar is defined in Internal.Bas, where 36 other functions are defined specific to Asvu.Exe. To see the code making up UnselVar, click on Internal.Bas in the **SysVars.Mak** dialogue box.

▸ The variable **SelHighlightedVar%** is a true/false bit. When set to true, then an AutoCAD system variable has been highlighted in LstVar list box.

▸ The procedure **ButOK_Click** displays the information about the AutoCAD system variable selected by the user.

LstVar_Click is not the only subroutine connected to LstVar. To see the other subroutines, click on the **Proc:** down arrow. The three actions in boldface also work with LstVar: DblClick, GotFocus, and ListFocus.

LstVar is not the only subroutine tied to an object. To see the other objects, click on the **Object:** down arrow. You see about 30 other subroutines, each of which has one or more procedures attached.

Interfacing with AutoCAD

In Release 11 for Windows, Visual Basic 1 programs communicate with AutoCAD via DDE. In Release 12, Visual Basic 2 programs communicate via ADS, the AutoCAD development system. ADS communicates via DDE with AutoLISP, which in turn communicates via DDE with AutoCAD.

The DDE Interface

Here is how to get a Visual Basic program to interact with AutoCAD via DDE, the Windows dynamic data exchange facility. The subroutines to set up the DDE link are as follows:

```
Sub LinkApp (Link as Control, AppName as String, Topic
    as String)
  Link.LinkMode=NONE
  Link.LinkTopic=AppName + "|" + Topic
  Link.LinkMode=COLD
End Sub

Sub Form_Load()
  LinkApp AcadText, "AutoCAD", "System"
End Sub
```

Let's look at the code in these two subroutines, line by line:

```
Sub LinkApp (Link as Control, AppName as String, Topic
    as String)
```

The first subroutine is called LinkApp. It creates a DDE link to any program, including AutoCAD. You can use this subroutine to link Visual Basic to any other DDE-aware Windows program, such as Excel or Write.

The subroutine defines three arguments, Link, AppName, and Topic, which it expects to have passed to it by other subroutines calling it:

▸ The argument Link is defined as a control. A *control* argument can operate on any kind of control passed to it. Later, you will see that the control "AcadText" is passed to LinkApp.

▸ The arguments AppName and Topic are defined as strings. Later, you will see that the strings "AutoCAD" and "System" are passed to LinkApp.

The LinkMode command (or *property*, as Visual Basic calls it) determines the kind of DDE link (hot or cold) and sets up the communications link. There are three steps to creating the DDE link between the Visual Basic program and AutoCAD:

1. The first step in establishing a DDE link is to ensure that no link exists:

```
Link.LinkMode=NONE
```

Setting LinkMode to 0 or to NONE ensures that any existing DDE communications that this program is involved in are shut down. Linkmode is associated with the form AcadText via argument Link.

2. The second step is to establish the link by specifying the name and topic of the application with the LinkTopic command. Later, you will see that the AppName argument holds "AutoCAD" and that the Topic argument holds "System." The vertical bar (|) acts as a separator between the application name and the topic name:

```
Link.LinkTopic=AppName + "|" + Topic
```

System is a special topic name in the world of DDE. Sending the "system" as a topic lets you make enquiries of the other program, such as what data formats it supports. What the system topic allows differs among Windows applications; for AutoCAD, the system topic allows you to send AutoCAD commands--a form of remote computing.

3. The third step is to specify the kind of DDE link:

```
Link.LinkMode=COLD
```

The 2 (or COLD) setting is equivalent to Excel's Warm setting: update communications only occur when requested (via the LinkRequest command). The 1 (or HOT) setting performs automatic updates each time the data changes.

The constants NONE and COLD are defined in Global.Bas, which contains the following line of code:

```
Global Const NONE=0, COLD=2
```

As I mentioned earlier, the LinkApp subroutine can be used to create a DDE link between any Visual Basic program and any other DDE-aware Windows program. It's the Form_Load subroutine that makes the DDE link with AutoCAD, as follows:

```
Sub Form_Load()
```

The Form_Load subroutine uses the Load command (an *event*, according to Visual Basic terminology) to automatically load the form. You can think of Form_Load as a kind of AutoExec.Bat file (which automatically loads when you turn on the computer) that automatically loads when you first run a Visual Basic program. In the world of Visual Basic, you use Form_Load to include initialization code in a form:

```
LinkApp AcadText, "AutoCAD", "System"
```

Here the job of Form_Load is defined: to automatically run LinkApp, the subroutine described above. Form_Load passes the parameters AcadText, "AutoCAD" and "System" to the LinkApp subroutine (recall that LinkApp establishes the DDE link with AutoCAD). AcadText is passed as a *control* parameter to LinkApp, so that LinkApp know which form to use for DDE communications.

If you want a Visual Basic program to run with another application, you can borrow these two subroutines. LinkApp can remain unchanged, while in Form_Load you change the "AutoCAD" to the name to the other program.

The ADS Interface

To help you create a Visual Basic application that communicates with AutoCAD via ADS, Release 12 includes six files to help you out. Subdirectory \Acadwin\Vb\New contains the following files, some of which you will recognize from the files used with Asvu.Exe:

- AdsFuncs.Bas is the BASic code that defines ADS functions

- AdsFuncs.Frm is the invisible FoRM for the ADS functions

- Global.Bas is the BASic code that defines global variables

- New.Frm is the FoRM file with which you start a new ADS-compatible Visual Basic application

- New.Mak is the MAKe file that groups these files together.

Summary
This chapter introduced you to methods of programming in Visual Basic. The next chapter describes several extensions to AutoCAD for Windows links with Visual Basic and programming aids.

Programming
Utilities

*I*n addition to utility programs supplied by third-party programmers, Autodesk has released additional software after the AutoCAD for Windows Releases 11 and 12 began shipping. This chapter describes these extra utilities that provide an AEW ADS extension for Turbo C++, additional Visual Basic functions, more icons for the Toolbar, and other programming environments.

Executive Summary

Utilities for Release 11:

- PdxEhg is the AutoCAD Windows to Paradox DOS transfer utility

- WinAdsTc is the ADS library for Turbo C++

- FindAcad.Dll provides additional AWE-specific Visual Basic functions

- Tbar32.Dll contains additional Toolbar icons

Utilities for Release 12:

- Spanner, from CAD Tools, is an Excel import program

- ProtoBox, from CAD Resource Center, is an aid to creating AutoCAD dialogue boxes

- Bitmaps, how-to-add bitmap icons to AutoCAD for Windows

- WinBlank, a getting-started guide to Windows ADS programming

The utility programs, along with support files, source code, and original documentation, are available on the optional diskette. See the back of this book for ordering information.

The Paradox Interface

One of the strengths of a CAD system is its links with database software, something AutoCAD has traditionally been weak in. The dynamic data exchange facility provided by Windows lets AutoCAD Release 11 finally create the links fairly easily.

PdxEhg.Exe is an ADS application that lets you exchange drawing data between AutoCAD Release 11 for Windows and Paradox v3.5 for DOS. The program uses the Paradox Engine v2.0 to manipulate the data. Database support is included with AutoCAD Release 12 via the ASE (AutoCAD SQL extension) and ASI (AutoCAD SQL interface)—and SQL is short for structured query language.

The PdxEhg program provides Release 11 two commands: Pdxout and Pdxin.

Pdxout exports table data from AutoCAD to the Paradox datafile file in a format that closely resembles ASCII DXF format. The AutoCAD table data is stored as Paradox tables with primary key files.

The Paradox tables are given a hybrid name, consisting of the first four characters of the AutoCAD drawing name, followed by an underscore and a three-character table identifier. For example, the Sample.Dwg file's layer table would be called SAMP_LAY in Paradox. The tables exported by Pdxout (with Paradox identifier) are:

- Entities (_ENT)
- Layers (_LAY)
- Linetypes (_LTY)
- Application IDs (_AID)
- Text styles (_STY)
- Viewports (_VPT)
- Dimension styles (_DIM)
- Views (_VEW)
- Named UCS (_UCS)
- Named blocks (_BLK)
- System variables (_SYS)

Once the tables have been exported to Paradox, you can use Paradox's database and programming capabilities to manipulate the information.

Pdxin imports the table information from Paradox to AutoCAD Release 11, with the exception of the viewport tables (_VPT). The command prompts you as follows:

```
Command: pdxin
Enter the name of the Paradox table: samp_lay
```

Type in the hybrid name, such as SAMP_LAY to retrieve the layer tables associated with the Sample.Dwg. The files included with the Paradox interface utility are:

- Pdxehg.Exe   The ADS application

- Pdxehg.C   C-language source code

- Pdxehg.H   DXF-definition include file

- Pdxehg.Mak   Make file for Microsoft C v6.00AX

- Pdxehg.Def   Module definition file

- Pdxehg.Rc   Icon resource compile file

- Paradox.Doc Brief documentation

At the time of Release 11, Autodesk had anticipated releasing another version of the Pdxehg utility once Paradox for Windows was released by Borland International. However, Release 12's SQL support superseded the need.

The ADS Library for Turbo C++

At the time of its release, the AutoCAD Release 11 Extension for Windows included support files for creating ADS applications for Microsoft C, Turbo C++, and Quick C for Windows.

WinAdsTc.Lib is the ADS library that lets you create Release 11 ADS applications with Borland International's Turbo C++ object-oriented programming language. Release 12 for Windows includes support for Turbo C++ and six other compilers.

The documentation accompanying WinAdsTc.Lib describes how to set up a Turbo C++ project file to create ADS applications that work with AcadWin. Also included is a modified version of WinUtil.C, the modeless toolbox application. The modified source code corrects one line code that causes the Turbo C++ compiler to complain.

The files included with the Turbo C++ ADS package are:

▸ WinAdsTc.Lib   ADS library file for Turbo C++

▸ WinUtil.C   C-language source code for Toolbox palette

▸ TurboC.Doc   Brief documentation

As with the DOS version of AutoCAD, Autodesk may well provide support for other Windows-based programming environments, in addition to Microsoft C, Quick C for Windows, and Turbo C++.

Additional Visual Basic Functions

Some versions of Visual Basic 1 appear to missing code mentioned in VB's reference manuals. Autodesk programmer Mark Hayes wrote FindAcad.DLL to add the three functions. Visual Basic 2, supported by Release 12 for Windows, includes Focus functions.

The functions—FindAcad, FindAcadText, and AcadActive—help to find and set focus to AutoCAD's drawing and text windows. *Focus* is a Visual Basic term. It refers to the ability of a part of a Visual Basic program to receive user input that is typed at the keyboard. For example, you use the **<Tab>** key to move the *focus* to different input fields and buttons. The functions perform the following:

hWnd FindAcad(void)	Returns a handle to the AcadWin drawing window
hWnd FindAcadText(void)	Returns a handle to AcadWin Text window
void AcadActive(hWnd)	Sets the focus to the window referenced by the handle

The three functions use *hWnd* (handles to Windows) in the FindAcad.Dll dynamic link library. A *handle* in Visual Basic is like a handle in AutoCAD: it is a unique ID number defined by the operating system. In Windows, handles refer to programs (as opposed to entities in AutoCAD). Although handles are integers, you cannot perform math functions on them.

Once the functions locate and focus on AutoCAD, you can send keystroke commands from Visual Basic to AcadWin with the SendKeys statement.

Additional Toolbar Icons

Autodesk provided a very limited set of icons in Release 11 for the pop-down menus and the Toolbar. Making your own icons isn't easy, either. But third-party developers are beginning to provide icon libraries.

The first is from Ken Billing, who created six Toolbar icons—in full color—that represent the most-common dialog boxes (see Figure). From left to right, the icons represent:

▶ Ddatte   the attribute editor

▶ Ddedit   the text editor

▶ Ddemodes   the entity creation dialog box

▶ Ddlmodes   the layer control dialog box

▶ Ddrmodes   the drawing control dialog box

▶ Dducs   the UCS control dialog box

When you assign these icons to the Toolbar, you won't see their names in the pop-down list. Instead, you need to type their name in the Bitmap ID text entry window.

File Link between Excel and AutoCAD

Wisbeck & Fraser CADtools
10827 NE Second Place
Bellevue, WA 98004

Spanner ($75), from CADtools, is a file utility that lets AutoCAD Release 12 read Excel spreadsheets. The file approach lets Spanner create tables in drawings using AutoCAD's lines (see Figure), which the Clipboard doesn't allow.

Spanner consists of an Excel macro (compatible with Excel v3 and v4) and an AutoLISP routine. The Span12.Xls macro writes the current worksheet to a X2A file on disk. It has a useful option that automatically writes the X2A file each time you close the worksheet. You are limited to having 100 characters per cell. Wrapped text is not wrapped in AutoCAD.

AutoCAD's special characters (such as %%d for the degree symbol) can be used in Excel.

The file format is an intermediate format (not an XLS file) that is read by the Span12.Lsp routine.

In AutoCAD, Span12.Lsp's dialogue box lets you specify the text font, color and layer for the four standard font styles (regular, bold, italic, and bold italic). You can also specify the color, width, linetype, layer, and visibility of Excel's grid and border lines. Cell shading and charts are not supported. After inserting the worksheet into the drawing, the Lisp routine lets you change the column width and row height. An amazing feature lets you dynamically pick new column widths. Use the AutoCAD Scale command to resize the worksheet.

Spanner does not reexport the AutoCAD table back into Excel, although this may be possible with a bit of DDE programming. Since Spanner uses an intermediate file, it can be used with the DOS version of Release 12. Still, it would be possible to set up a DDE link to automate the process of creating Excel-based tables in AutoCAD for Windows.

Prototyping Software for Dialogue Boxes

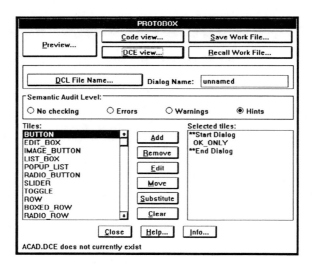

CAD Resource Center
77 Progress Ave., Suite 201
Scarborough, ON M1P 2Y7

AutoCAD Release 12 introduced programmable dialogue boxes via DCL, the dialogue control language. While a dialogue box written with DCL works with any version of Release 12, Autodesk did not provide any programming tools. Unlike other Windows-based programming environments that let you create a dialogue box by simply placing elements, you have to write the code the hard way.

ProtoBox ($50; shareware), from the CAD Resource Center, lets you create dialogue boxes for AutoCAD in much the same way as Visual Basic and Excel's Dialog Editor. You select and place components (such as buttons and sliders), and ProtoBox writes the DCL code that AutoCAD requires (see Figure) Since ProtoBox takes take of the DCL coding, you don't need to be expert in *yet another* AutoCAD programming language.

With ProtoBox, you can add the following 25 objects to an AutoCAD dialogue box:

```
Boxed_column, Boxed_radio_column, Boxed_radio_row,
Boxed_row, Button
Column, Comment
Edit_box, Errtile
Image, Image_button
List_box
Ok_cancel, Ok_cancel_help, Ok_cancel_help_info,
Ok_only
Popup_list
Radio_button, Radio_column, Radio_row, Row
Slider, Spacer
Text, Toggle
```

When AutoCAD reads a DCL file, it checks for errors and places the errors in a DCE error file. ProtoBox lets you set one of AutoCAD's four error checking levels: no checking, error checking, warning checking, and redundant attribute checking. ProtoBox includes the following files:

▸ ProtoBox.Lsp is the ProtoBox program, written in AutoLISP

▸ ProtoBox.Dcl defines the Protobox dialogue box

▸ ProtoBox.Hlp is the help file, which also provides the documentation

Writing Bitmaps for Release 12

The software package Bitmap.Zip contains instructions for adding bitmaps to Tbar16.Dll and Tbar24.Dll. These two dynamic link libraries contain the icons used by the Toolbar and Toolbox. Tbar16 contains smaller icons, 16x16 pixels in size; Tbar24 contains larger icons, 24 x 24 pixels in size.

The ZIP file contains Bitmap.Bat, a batch file that builds a new version of the two DLLs. Instructions are given in Bitmap.Doc on how to use Microsoft C/C++, Borland C/C++, and the Borland Resource Workshop. Bitmap.Zip contains the following files:

- Bitmap.Bat is the batch file for Microsoft C/C++
- BitmapBc.Bat is the batch file for Borland C/C++
- TBar16.C, TBar24.C, TBar16.Def, and TBar24.Def are used during the build
- TBar16.Rc and TBar24.Rc contain the list of BMP files to be included in the DLLs

Bitmap.Zip also contains 168 BMP files. Whereas AutoCAD Release 12 for Windows comes with the icons as 16 x 16-pixel BMP files, it does not include the 24 x 24 pixel BMP files. The ZIP file contains all icons in both sizes.

Getting-Started Guide
to Windows ADS Programming

WinBlank is a collection of files that helps budding ADS programmers get started in the Widows programming environment. The sample applications displays a dialogue box and stores information about it in the initialization file WinBlank.Ini.

The WinBlank.C source code file (about four pages worth) contains the code common to all ADS applications, which can be used as a prototype for creating your own ADS applications. In addition, WinBlank.C contains the code for the sample Windows dialogue box. WinBlank implements two commands: (1) Sample displays the dialogue box; (2) Sample2 lists all blocks with constant attributes.

The documentation includes instructions for compiling WinBlank with Borland Turbo C++ 3.0, Microsoft QuickC for
Windows and Microsoft C 6.0. WinAds.Zip contains the following files:

- ▸ WinBlank.C   Sample ADS program displays dialogue box

- ▸ WinBlank.Rc   Resource definition file that defines dialogue boxes, icons, menu bars, and strings

- ▸ WinBlank.Def   Link definition file

- ▸ WinBlank.Dlg   Defines the dialogue box

- ▸ WinBlank.Ico A simple icon for use with the WinBlank application

- ▸ WinAdsQc.Lib   ADS library file for Quick C

- ▸ WinAdsBc.Lib   ADS library file for Turbo C++

- ▸ WinAds.Lib   ADS library file for MicroSoft C

Index

Diskette Order Form

All the shareware mentioned in this book is available on diskette. Use the form on this page to place your order. Do not order diskettes from Delmar Publishers. This offer is only available from the author. Some programs are shareware that require payment of a registration fee. To obtain commercial software mentioned in this book, contact the vendor directly.

- -

Circle Your Selection

Disk	Description	Price
1	Chapter 8: LoadMon, Graphic Viewer, Graphic Workshop, PixFolio, Bmp2Dxf, Task Tracker, Lister, and WinDump.	$5.00
2	Chapter 9: Audio Notes, Wave Editor, and PC speaker driver for Windows.	$5.00
3	Chapter 10: Animation Tool Kit and Animation Player for Windows.	$5.00
4	Chapter 16: PdxEhg, WinAdsTc.Lib, FindAcad.Dll, Toolbr, Protobox, and Bitmap.Zip.	$5.00

Total order $

Indicate diskette size: **5-1/4" 3-1/2"** Make cheque payable to **Ralph Grabowski**. US and international orders: prices are in US funds. Canadian orders: prices are in Canadian funds. Canadian residents add 7% GST. GST registration number: R133285619.

Shipping Information

Ship to: _____

Address: _____

City, State, Code, Country: _____

Mail your order to:
CAD Visions, P.O. Box 3053, Sumas, WA 98295-3053
Allow four to six weeks for delivery.